BRIGHTER DAYS

100 Thoughts of Hope, Love and Blessings

Thanks for your Support

Eziaku

July 4 2024

BRIGHTER DAYS

100 Thoughts of Hope, Love and Blessings

EZIAKU ODIMUKO

CONTENTS

To my husband, with love.

FORWARD

I am very pleased to write the forward to this fascinating inspirational book, "Brighter Days", in which Eziaku shares her collection of personal inspirational thoughts and meditations that bring hope and blessings to everyone. Eziaku is a woman of God who gives genuinely; be it financially, material, or spiritual gifts which she receives from the Lord. I have had the privilege to be the first to read this book, and I realized that one of her giftings, which is in the area of giving, is well displayed in her willingness to share the secrets of financial breakthroughs, good relationships, and unmovable faith through her personal devotion.

This book will take you on a journey of discovery into the lives and experiences of great men and women of the Bible who have gone through pain, trials, and rough times, but through faith in the Word, have found joy, peace, and hope. You will also discover your identity and true value in life because meditation produces a chance to draw from the wisdom of God. As Isaiah 33:6 puts it, "the knowledge you acquire from the Scriptures will give you depth and stability in your days." This leads to spiritual tasting of the Scripture, character growth-to fruit, success, direction, and happiness.

Again, David, the man after God's own heart points in Psalm 1:3 that the Christian who "meditates day and night on the Word of God shall be like a tree planted by the rivers of water. That tree will yield its fruit in season, and its leaves will not wither".

As you spend time meditating on the chapters of this book, your courage will not fail, your faith will increase, and you will begin to walk in humility before God, resulting in creating a spiritual sensitivity to hear from God, the Creator of heavens and the earth. Every word in this book is filled with God's anointing. It comes directly from a pure heart.

I believe Eziaku has written these personal inspirational thoughts and meditations by the direction of the Lord. It is her sincere desire that you should be blessed. My prayer is, as you begin reading, God will cause you to enjoy *Brighter Days* in your own personal life, family, education, business, and in your home. God bless you.

Rose Donkor, PhD
Co-Senior Pastor
All Nations Full Gospel Churches International

Acknowledgement

I would like to thank all those who contributed to the success of the completion of *Brighter Days*.

A special thanks to my Senior Pastors, Drs. Samuel and Rose Donkor, for their spiritual leadership and mentorship. Under their leadership and ministry, my family and I have grown immensely in our walk with God.

I wish to thank my lovely daughters Abigail, Esther and Sarah, for helping me throughout the process of writing this book, for always being available for me to bounce off ideas, for their patience as I worked on this project and for helping me with the title of this book. Thank you to my mom, Lady Rhoda Anyanwu, for her love and continued support as I worked on this project. Thank you to my parents-in-law, Dr. Chijioke and Lady Elizabeth Odimuko, for their love and support as I worked on this project. Thanks to my brother, Dr. David Anyanwu, for providing constructive input towards the success of this project. Thanks to my entire family, who encouraged me and cheered me along as I worked on this project.

My gratitude also goes to my friend, Kate Otomewo, for always encouraging me and making herself available to pick her brain and come up with great ideas as I thought about this book's title.

I am forever grateful to David Ngoka and the team at Vida ICT Solutions for their immense help in bringing this project to reality, from working on the cover page to creating amazing designs and websites, all geared towards the creation and publishing of this book. I'm also indebted to Jason and Vidya with the team @ ebookpbook for editing the book's manuscript and working with me to finalize Brighter Days' creation.

Special thanks go to my husband, Dike, for his love and support throughout the process of producing *Brighter Days*, for providing additional edits and helping to bring this work to life; and to the board, leadership and members of All Nations Full Gospel Church Edmonton for their continued love and support.

Finally, I want to thank God for His love and blessings in my life.

INTRODUCTION

Are you tired of the negative news all around? Have you been worn down and depressed by challenges all around? Do you worry about the hopelessness that is palpable in the world? Are you saddened by racial inequality, injustice and the downward spiral of society? Are you caught in between a murky past and a gloomy tomorrow? Do your days feel dull and drab? Do you want to experience brighter days?

Brighter Days is a book of hope, love and blessings. It takes you on a journey of discovery into the lives and stories of people who have come through pain to find joy and hope in God. It brings you thoughts and lessons from the lives of others who have found hope, love and blessings in God. *Brighter Days* is your companion to enjoy confidence in your everyday. It brings you inspiration, cheer and comfort using easily understood bible verses thoughtfully woven into everyday life stories.

Brighter Days is a compilation of 100 inspirational reflections that I have had the privilege to discover in God's word during my time of personal meditation. This book is written in a way that will build up your ability to study God's word for yourself. This collection of hope-filled reflections is very personal because I recall the joy of being inspired and strengthened in those moments.

As an author, banker, mom, daughter and pastor's wife, I understand how important it is to find hope and strength for everyday living. I have served in ministry alongside my husband for seventeen years, helping, encouraging and empowering people from different walks of life. I genuinely enjoy bringing hope to others, be it in their financial life, relationships, or spiritual walk. My first book, *Relationship Smart: Love, Courtship and Marriage*, was written to give help and guidance to young women as they go through their relationships.

I invite you to enjoy *Brighter Days*. It can be read through in a single sitting or used as a daily companion for your devotion time. My hope is that your days are filled with the brightness that comes as a result of renewed hope in God. No more dreading gloomy days; let's get you ready and looking ahead to brighter days!

I

An Extraordinary Love

Ruth 1:16
But Ruth said, entreat me not to leave you, or to turn back from following after you, for wherever you go, I will go, and wherever you lodge, I will lodge. Your people shall be my people, and your God, my God.

Have you experienced love that was so genuine and loyal that you wondered what you did to deserve it? This was the kind of love that Ruth showed her mother-in-law, Naomi. Naomi had lost her husband and two sons, one of who had been married to Ruth. She found herself destitute, widowed and bereaved of her sons. Life for Naomi seemed hopeless. She pleaded with her daughters-in-law, Ruth and Orpah, to go back to their families and start a new life. She explained that she had nothing more to offer them and that life with her had no hope in sight. In response, Ruth made a passionate plea of love and commitment, promising to remain with Naomi no matter what life brought their way!

Ruth's love and commitment to Naomi remind me of the extraordinary love Jesus has for us. He remains committed to us, promising never to leave us nor to forsake us, despite our shortcomings. Like Naomi, though we may feel unworthy, yet we can be confident in the steadfast and dependable love of God. We can have hope in difficult times because of the love that God has for us. God loves you, and He wants to bless your life. God's love and mercies are not for a privileged few. They are for you too. You can experience the love that is in Christ Jesus. No one can stop you from experiencing this divine love.

I have enjoyed unconditional love from my parents and siblings. After I got married, I continued to receive this love from my husband and children. It is indeed a blessing to enjoy the love of family, but I can truly say that nothing is more satisfying than the love that God gives. God's love is always available to you, even when the love of family is absent.

2

LIFE'S TROUBLES CAN TAKE US TO A BAD PLACE

Ruth 1:2
And they went to the country of Moab and remained there.

Where has life's trouble taken you? Where have life's challenges kept you? It is one thing to go through difficulty, trouble, pain, trials or challenges, and it is another thing to remain in the place of pain and sorrow. Naomi's tragedies took her to a place of anger and bitterness toward God. The name Naomi in Hebrew means "pleasant," delightful. Where has the trouble of life taken you spiritually? Are you in a place of sorrow, bitterness and anger toward God? Are you in a place of unbelief, unforgiveness, depression and doubt?

> *"But she said to them, 'Do not call me Naomi; call me Mara for the Almighty has dealt very bitterly with me'"* (Ruth 1:20).

Satan is the author of pain. God is the healer. *"The thief does not come except to steal, and to kill, and to destroy. I have come that they may have life and that they may have it more abundantly"* (John 10:10).

When I lost my dad many years ago, I felt very sad and had many questions. Though I did not have all the answers, I could trust God to heal my heart and comfort me. When we face pain, loss or disappointments, the devil always wants us to attribute it to God. He tries to get us to be mad at God. If you have been through a terrible situation, know that God wants to help you and not hurt you. He wants to bless you, not destroy you. Come out from the place of anger toward God because He loves you and will help you.

3

TIME TO RISE UP AND MOVE FORWARD

Ruth 1:6-7
Then she arose with her daughters-in-law that she might return from
the country of Moab, for she had heard in the country of Moab that
the Lord had visited His people by giving them bread. Therefore, she
went out from the place where she was, and her two daughters' in law
with her; and they went on the way to return to the land of Judah.

What do you do when you hear of God's faithfulness and His goodness
to others? When you hear of God's goodness, allow it to build your faith.
Naomi arose and returned. You must not remain in the place of sorrow
and bitterness. Take a step of faith towards hope.

The road to turning to God is sometimes filled with discouragement. Loved ones may discourage you, like Naomi discouraged Orpah.
"Turn back, my daughters. Why will you go with me?" (Ruth 1: 11). It takes
faith and determination to move toward a place of hope. Do not let people discourage you. Choose to move forward in hope and leave your past
behind!

Discouragement can also come from within us. Reasoning about a
situation and making sense of things can sometimes prevent us from
looking ahead in hope. Let us always keep in mind that God is not

limited by the things that limit us. He can turn things around for you if you continue to have hope and trust in Him. Every day is an opportunity to experience new blessings. We must remain hopeful and expect good things. I used to worry about mistakes of the past, but with encouragement and understanding, I have come to know that holding on to the past will only prevent me from taking hold of the future. God does not want you to live in the past. He wants you to rise up and move forward.

4

TOUGH TIMES CALL FOR TOUGH FAITH

Romans 8:35
Who shall separate us from the love of Christ? Shall tribulation, or
distress, or persecution, or famine, or nakedness, or peril, or sword?

Tough times are not fun times. One of such challenging times for my family was when my dad lost his job. As a result of the job loss, the family went through a season of lack where it was hard for my parents to put food on the table. They also struggled to pay tuition for my siblings, some of whom were in universities at the time. There were times my sister and I would cook but barely have anything left over for both of us to eat. But somehow, I never saw my dad complain. As a family, we were joyful and content, and if we never told you, you would never know that things were hard. My dad's faith in God did not waver, and he remained committed to the things of God like he did when things were good. He did not let the lack we faced as a family separate us from God's love.

Are you facing a situation that makes you want to turn your back on God? We may not always know how we will react in times of difficulty, but we can rely on and be confident that nothing will separate us from the love Christ has for us. Though we may falter in our faith, yet we can trust in the One who remains forever faithful. The Lord is committed to you. He has promised never to leave you nor forsake you. He loves you. When you face tough times, trust in Him. Have hope in Him, and He will see you through.

When our faith is not strong and bold, we can ask the Lord for grace to love Him more and more each day. I pray that when you face a challenge that tests your faith, you will stand firm and proclaim your love for the Lord.

5

God's Got Your Back!

Ruth 2:1
There was a relative of Naomi's husband, a man of great wealth, of
the family of Elimelech. His name was Boaz.

When Satan thought he had done his worst to Ruth and Naomi, killing their family members and destroying their lives, little did he know that God had another plan for these women. You see, God is always ahead of the enemy. When the enemy closes one door of success to you, God opens up another! He restores hope to the hopeless. Someone once said, "God has a million ways to solve one problem." Don't let the problems you face discourage you. God is already working a way out for you. He is putting together a plan to confuse, perplex and confound the enemy.

Ruth thought that her only living relative was Naomi. She thought all hope was lost to her being able to get married, raise children and have a family, but thanks be to God, *"There was a relative..."*

Has the enemy thrown a curveball at your plans? Do you find yourself questioning how to make sense of it all? Remember, it is not over until God says so. He has the master plan for your life and will make a way for you. As Ruth discovered *a relative,* may you discover Jesus Christ, your Savior, high priest, brother, friend, redeemer, and so much more. Cheer up, my friend! God's got your back! May He continually open new doors of opportunities for you in Jesus' name!

6

When Your Steps Are Ordered

Ruth 2:3
Then she left and went and gleaned in the field after the reapers. And she happened to come to the part of the field belonging to Boaz, who was of the family of Elimelech.

When I got accepted to the Federal University of Technology, Owerri, to study Industrial Microbiology, little did I know that God was ordering my steps. My initial plan was to spend the first year in the school and transfer out to another university to study Medicine, but God had other plans for me. Not only did I not transfer out, I completed my program and also met my best friend who was studying Civil Engineering in the same school. He would later become my husband! God guides your steps. There is no happenstance with God's children. He will order every step of yours if only you will trust Him.

When Ruth went out to glean in the field that fateful morning, little did she know that God was ordering her steps! The Bible says, *"And she happened to come to the part of the field belonging to Boaz."*

As a child of God, do you know that your steps are ordered by the Lord? Do you know that you are important to God, and He is in control of your life? A scripture I love so much is found in *Romans 8:28: "And we know that all things work together for good to those who love God, to those who are the called according to His purpose."*

Stop panicking. Your life is in God's hands. Trust Him to order your steps. Learn to commit all your plans to Him, and then trust Him to lead and direct you. There may be times you don't understand the path He is taking you on; simply trust and know that in the end, it will work out for your good. May God order your steps, and may He direct your path.

7

REDEEMED

Ruth 4:13
So Boaz took Ruth and she became his wife.

Marriage takes two people and makes them one. You notice, Boaz could have kept providing Ruth with daily provisions, but the ultimate blessing would be that of redeeming her to himself to become his wife. By taking Ruth to become his wife, Boaz could freely share all that he had with her. She was no longer a mere stranger or a maidservant, but she was brought into a beautiful union of love and companionship with Boaz through marriage.

This is similar to what Christ Jesus has done for you and me through His sacrifice on the cross. Before, we were strangers to God, but through Christ's redemptive work, we are no longer strangers; rather, we have become sons and daughters of God. God's greatest blessing to humankind is that of redemption. Jesus has redeemed us, and now we are His.

"For you were bought at a price; therefore, glorify God in your body and in your spirit, which are God's." (1Corinthians 6:20)

Jesus has paid the price for our redemption. He has taken us, the church, to be His bride, just like Boaz took Ruth to become his wife. He wants to bring you into a close union with Him. Will you leave behind the pain, anger, hurt, bitterness, abuse and rejection of the past and embrace the one who wants to restore you to God's original plan and purposes for your life? God is ready to work a miracle in your life. He loves you more than you know. You are His beloved.

8

One Woman's Encounter with Jesus

John 4:4
But he needed to go through Samaria.

When we were courting, my husband would always travel from the city where he lived with his parents to come to visit me. It was a journey of about sixty-two kilometers, and because he didn't have a car, he would take public transport, which was no picnic. He told me how important those visits were to him and how he would work arduous jobs to save up some money just so that he could come to visit and spend time with me. He was happy to visit every week and sometimes more than once or twice a week!

Jesus needed to go through Samaria because He had a divine appointment with the Samaritan woman. Jesus chose to go on a grueling journey to meet this woman who needed His help. Jesus is willing to walk longer, harder and farther just to meet with you, to encounter you and to change your life. Remember, this woman was a Samaritan, and Samaritans were despised by the Jews. She also had troubled relationships. She had five husbands and lived with a sixth man who was not her husband! I imagine she must have been the talk of the village! The other women must have gossiped about her. All that notwithstanding, Jesus went through Samaria because of her.

It does not matter where you are right now. It does not matter what you have been through or what other people think or say about you. Jesus does not need anyone's permission to help you. Stop worrying about what people are saying about you. It does not matter what people think or say about you. Hold on to your Lord who loves you. Know that Jesus loves you. He cares for you, and He is reaching out to you right now.

9

BLESSED LOVE

2 Samuel 1:26
Your love to me was wonderful.

What blessed love Christ has for me. It is stronger than any love I have ever experienced.

Friend, have you experienced this love? *"For God so loved the world, that He gave His only begotten Son, that whoever believes in Him should not perish but have everlasting life" (John 3:16).* His love does not condemn. It sets free. It says, *"Neither do I condemn you. Go and sin no more!" (John 8:11).*

His love is not partial. It is open to all. It is available to you. Your past does not hinder it. Your present does not hamper it. His love is patient and true. This is love that you can truly trust. Love that sets free. Love like nothing you have known before. *"Since you were precious in My sight, you have been honored and I have loved you. Therefore, I will give men for you, and people for your life" (Isaiah 43:4).*

Your love, oh Lord, to me is wonderful.
Great love, greater than Jonathan's.
Deep love, deeper than the mighty sea.
Forgiving love, speaking better things than Abel's blood.
Fascinating love, drawing me ever so closely to you.

Your love to me is wonderful.
Sacrificial love, giving your life for me.
Blessed love, reaching far and wide,
high and low, deep and vast.
Your love, oh Lord, to me is wonderful,
surpassing the love of men.

10

Jesus Knows and Wants to Deal with Your Secrets

John 4:16
Go, call your husband, and come here.

Sometimes my youngest daughter will whisper something in my ears, taking care to make sure her sisters don't hear. She will say to me, "Mommy, it's my secret. You can't tell anyone."

"Okay," I will reply, getting ready to hear the secret, "I won't tell anyone!"

Secrets. Everyone has them. However, there is one person who knows how to help us with all the secrets of our hearts. Jesus understands everything we have been through; He knows our strengths and weakness, and there is nothing hidden from Him. He wants to deal with our secrets so that He can heal us from the scars, sorrows, hurts and pains of our sinful lives and free us to serve Him. No wonder He said to the Samaritan woman, *"Go, call your husband."*

Why did Jesus ask the Samaritan woman to go and call her husband? Did Jesus not know that she had many husbands? Of course, Jesus knew her personal circumstances just as He knows ours. What are the things that have happened to you that have brought you nightmares, guilt, sorrow, shame, pain and sickness? What are those things that make you hide your face and lower your head in shame? Share your secrets with the Lord in prayer.

Today, you can bring your problems to God. You can open up and share your secrets with the One who can take your mess and create a beautiful message out of it. Our Lord knows everything and will restore you so that you can be free to love and serve Him. You never have to be afraid because He will say, *"Neither do I condemn you. Go and sin no more" (John 8:11)*.

I I

A Changed Life

John 4:29
Come, see a Man, who told me all things that I ever did.

This once *sin-stricken* woman has become an evangelist! Hallelujah! When we encounter Jesus, He turns our weakness to witnesses; He turns our pains to praise and our sorrows to singing. When was the last time you declared of the goodness of the Lord? When was the last time you called out to your friends and family and said to them, *"Come and see"*?

How often do we experience God's goodness and sit on it, hold on to it and refuse to tell others of the great mercies we received from the Lord? When we find ways to communicate our faith and testify to God's goodness and mercies to us, we grow in our faith. It is easy to find areas of our lives that God has strengthened and tell our family and friends about it.

The Samaritan woman did not allow her secrets, pains, fears, guilt and sorrows to hold her back. She quickly ran to the village and called out to the men to *come and see.* Your testimony is your story. No one can dispute the personal experience you have had in your life. Have you been healed of a sickness? Have you overcome a sin? Have the weak areas of your life been strengthened? Has the Lord helped you with your academics, marriage, life or career? In what ways have you been blessed? How has the Lord changed your life? Remember, you don't have to sit on your testimonies. You can share with family and friends and say, *"Come and see"*

12

But You Shall
Receive Power

Acts 1:8
But you shall receive power when the Holy Spirit has come upon you.

Receiving the Holy Spirit was so important that Jesus commanded His disciples not to leave Jerusalem but to wait for the promise of the Father. Every child of God needs the Holy Spirit. I was in one of our church's retreat when God gave me a revelation on this verse. The disciples thought Jesus was referring to the restoration of political authority and power to Israel at that time, so they asked Jesus, *"Lord, will you at this time restore the kingdom to Israel?" (Acts1: 6b).*

The Holy Spirit is *not* given for political authority. The Holy Spirit is *not* for gaining knowledge that God has withheld from us. The Holy Spirit is not given for us to seek knowledge of things that God has expressly forbidden us. The Holy Spirit is not for fortune-telling, nor is He given for spiritual showmanship. He is not given so that we can take pride in our intellectual or physical abilities, nor is He given that we may exercise control over others or manipulate others.

In contrast, the Holy Spirit is given to God's children to empower them to live godly lives that bear witness to Jesus Christ. The Holy Spirit enables God's children to shine their lights for Jesus. The Holy Spirit comes to make us able witnesses of Christ.

"But you shall receive power when the Holy Spirit has come upon you; and you shall be witnesses to Me in Jerusalem, and in all Judea and Samaria, and to the end of the earth" (Acts 1:8).

13

DISCOVERING YOUR IDENTITY AND TRUE VALUE

2 Corinthians 4:7
But we have this treasure in earthen vessels.

Who are you? What is your true value? Uncovering your identity will help you discover your true value. It will also help you discover your purpose and ultimately help you achieve success in your relationship with God and others.

There is something about you that is hard for others, and sometimes even you, to grasp. You are a treasure. Yes, despite the imperfections you have, there is a special treasure that is inside of you. A hidden treasure. A treasure so valued that it cost God His only begotten son. You are special; you are unique. You are God's beloved. Little wonder, David exclaimed in *Psalm 139:14 "I will praise thee; for I am fearfully and wonderfully made: marvelous are your works: and that my soul knows very well."*

God placed a value on you before you were born. Stop letting your circumstances undermine what you really are. Only your creator knows the value He has placed inside of you. You can uncover your true value by growing daily in your fellowship with your Heavenly Father.

Isaiah 43:1-7 "Fear not, for I have redeemed you; I have called you by name; you are Mine..."

1Peter 2:9 "But you are a chosen generation, a royal priesthood, a holy nation; His own special people..."

14

Identifying Yourself through Relationships

John 4:17
For you have had five husbands, and the one whom you now have is
not your husband.

When I think of unproductive relationships, I think of certain transport buses found in cities such as Lagos, Nigeria. These buses usually have a person called the *bus conductor*, whose job is to get passengers in and out of the bus and collect the bus fares. Unlike the bus driver or the passengers, the bus conductor has no destination. He just continues going in circles in the bus throughout the day while passengers get in and out to their destinations. This is simply how some relationships are. There is no destination, no purpose, no goal, and the participants just keep going in circles! The Samaritan woman identified herself through her relationships with men. She had many relationships, and she was never comfortable being alone. She lost herself to her relationships until she met Jesus.

How do your relationships define you? Relationships can sometimes be like elevators. They either take you up or down. In life, sometimes we have negative experiences in our relationships. Have you made mistakes? Jesus is willing to help you. Have you been used, abused or rejected? Jesus can heal you. Has your trust been shattered, your heart broken, or your body bruised? Jesus can gently mend your broken heart and heal your hurting soul. He wants to give you a new beginning.

Have you been told you are no good? Have you lost your identity? Jesus is waiting to tell you of His love for you, and He will help you reveal your worth to you. Let Him help you to see yourself as you truly should see—chosen and beloved.

15

THE LENS OF WEALTH

Luke 12:20
But God said to him, "Fool! This night your soul will be required of
you; then whose will those things be which you have provided?"
   This night, not tomorrow—a message to the rich fool. Money has
no power to buy you a tomorrow.
   This night, not tomorrow, an account, he must give.
   Oh mammon, what rich fool you have made of man.

Do you see yourself through the lens of wealth?

Are you driven by an excessive desire to accumulate more? What is your relationship with money? Do you love it? Do you value it above every other thing? Does the love of money rule your life?

Jesus has this for all of us: *"Take heed and beware of covetousness, for one's life does not consist in the abundance of the things he possesses"* (Luke 12:15).

King Solomon enjoyed excessive wealth, yet at the end of his life's quest, he concluded that it was better to *"Fear God and keep His commandments, for this is man's all. For God will bring every work into judgment, including every secret thing, whether good or bad"* (Ecclesiastes 12:13).

Take a moment and review your relationship with money. Does it serve your needs, or do you serve it? Remember, you can lay up treasures in heaven by using your resources to do God's will here on earth. Do not let money rule your life. Your life is worth much more.

16

ALONE WITH GOD

Genesis 32:24
And Jacob was left alone.

Oh, the beauty of time alone with God! Time to pour out your heart with tears and supplication or joy and appreciation. Time to be refreshed, when your heart is renewed with a peaceful assurance of God's infinite love for you. Times, oh the times of fresh revelations, divine discoveries, intimate vitality, powerful promises and unbreakable vows. Do you enjoy time alone with God?

Jacob had lived most of his life without a definite relationship with God. His life's circumstances had defined him. His name meant "trickster," and he was known as a swindler. He swindled his brother Esau and his uncle Laban, and he continued in his scheming ways until he reached a dead end. He only reclaimed his true identity when he found himself alone with God.

The Lord made you for a purpose and has brought you this far for a reason. Learn to spend time in daily devotion with God and watch as your life is transformed, one day at a time. Get into the habit of being alone with God in prayer and study of His word, for there you will grow in your walk with God.

Connect yourself to the body of Christ through a local church and watch yourself transform in your Christian walk. Learn to use your gifts to serve others. Time alone with God will help you grow.

17

DIVINE DIRECTION

Matthew 1:20
But while he thought about these things, behold an angel of the Lord
appeared to him in a dream.

Joseph found himself deliberating on a crucial decision. This was a decision of a lifetime. Should he secretly call off his relationship with his pregnant wife, Mary, or should he not? Some decisions demand a divine direction to keep us on the right path. Sometimes, God sees us musing and mulling over an issue, and He comes with an answer of direction through His word, in a dream or through godly counsel from a person.

Like Joseph, you can enjoy divine direction from the Lord Himself as you learn to spend time communing with Him. He not only hears your prayers, but He also sees and understands your thoughts. When you are confronted with an important decision, do not run around looking for answers everywhere; instead, go to God in prayer, and He will provide you with the right answer for your situation. He will surely lead and direct you.

God is in control of your life. *"The steps of a good man are ordered by the Lord, and he delights in his way" (Psalm 37: 23). "All things work together for good to those who love the Lord" (Romans 8:28).* God is never late. He is always on time. It doesn't matter what you are going through this season. I want you to know that God is in control.

God can also provide you with counsel through those around you. *"In the multitude of counselors there is safety" (Proverbs 11:14).* Do not let pride stop you from seeking the counsel you need.

18

Be Strong

Joshua 1:6
Be strong and of good courage.

Be strong! These two simple words can make a world of difference in our everyday lives. Are you about to take an exam? Be strong. Are you about to make a life-changing decision? Be strong. Are you about to take on a new task, a new challenge or a new assignment? Be strong.

How many opportunities have you passed by because of fear? How many decisions have you made or not made because of fear? In life, we need strength and courage to obey God at every turn. Strength and courage do not come from within us; instead, they come when we spend time in the word of God, day and night. It is in that exercise that we are given the grace *to do according to all that is written.*

> *This Book of the Law shall not depart from your mouth, but you shall meditate in it day and night, that you may observe to do according to all that is written in it. For then you will make your way prosperous and then you will have good success. (Joshua 1:8)*

God passionately urges His children not to be fearful.

Fear and faith cannot coexist. May the Holy Spirit uproot every fear in your life and empower you to be all that God has called you to be.

19

THE LIMITING POWER OF FEAR

2 Timothy 1:7
God has not given us a Spirit of fear.

Wherever there is sin, fear is usually not far away. Sin and fear go hand in hand. Adam was afraid once he sinned against God. He said, *"I heard the voice of God and I was afraid..." (Genesis 3:10).*

Fear causes us to sin against God time and time again. Fear hinders us from receiving our miracles. Fear cancels out our faith, and without faith, it is impossible to please God. God does not want us to be full of fear. He has not given us a spirit of fear.

Fear manifests itself in various forms—fear of people, fear of poverty, fear of the past, fear of the future, fear of being alone, fear of commitment, fear of death, fear of failure, fear of rejection, fear of so many different things. May God deliver you from any fear that plagues your life.

King Saul was a fearful man. Little wonder God rejected him. His fear of people made him constantly disobey God. Fear of people will hinder you from obeying God. Joshua was often commanded not to be afraid. You may find yourself being lured by others to disobey God. Do not let the fear of people make you displease God. Ask God to take away the spirit of fear from you. Ask to be filled with love, peace and a sound mind.

20

A New Thing

Isaiah 43:19
Behold, I will do a new thing.

Are you troubled by your past? Are you continually disturbed with thoughts of your past failures? Are you unable to move into your future because you are holding on to the past?

God's word says, "Behold, I do a new thing." Behold! See! To see, you have to look up. You have to look ahead and look onward to visualize the good things God has in store for you. Stop looking back and allowing your head to hang low; it's time to look up. It's time to anticipate the new blessings God is bringing your way! Look up, friend. Wipe your tears. Look up! Jesus invites you to look up to Him. He is the author and finisher of your faith. David knows a thing or two about looking up. He says in *Psalm 121:1-2* "*I will lift up my eyes to the hills. From whence comes my help. My help comes from the Lord, who made heaven and earth.*"

God has promised to do a new thing in your life; therefore, you can have hope and look forward to new blessings in all areas of your life. Today, choose to let go of the past and welcome new blessings of health, peace and joy. God is bringing new blessings your way. Rise up and embrace your blessings! Don't hold on to your past anymore.

Are you ready to let go of the past and let God into your future? Remember, fear and faith do not go hand in hand. If you want to enjoy what God has in store for you, you must be willing to look forward to the future with hope and faith, leaving the past where it belongs, behind.

21

GOD KNOWS YOU

Psalm 139: 1
Oh Lord, You have searched me and known me.

God knows you perfectly. He knows you deep down, inside out, upside down, round about. He has perfect, omniscient knowledge of all things and all people, including you and me. What an awesome God He is.

Have you ever known a person as much as the person knows you? God's knowledge of man is thorough, infinite and deep.

God's knowledge is perfect and protective and infinite. *"Before I formed thee in the belly, I knew thee; and before thou camest forth out of the womb I sanctified thee, and I ordained thee a prophet unto the nations" (Jeremiah 1:5).*

"You have hedged me behind and before and laid your hand upon me. Such knowledge is too wonderful for me; it is high, I cannot attain it" (Psalm 139: 5-6).

Though man's knowledge of God is very limited, we can be confident in God's knowledge of us.

God's knowledge of us should not scare us away; instead, it should draw us closer to Him each day.

God reveals more and more of Himself to us as we spend time in His word. May we, like Paul, cry out *"that I may know you and the power of your resurrection" (Philippians 3:10).*

22

GIVE ME A DRINK

John 4: 7
Jesus said to her, "Give Me a drink."

Jesus asked the Samaritan woman for a drink, but her response was that of disbelief. How could a Jew ask her, a Samaritan, for water? Are you amazed by what you feel the Lord is asking of you? Do you feel inadequate or lacking the ability to do what God wants you to do? The good news is that God knows our weaknesses, and He wants to help us. He will never ask us to do something that He has not granted us the ability or the grace to do.

Whenever the Lord asks you for something, it is because He is getting ready to bless you with something far better. We can either give excuses, or we can trust His direction and guidance. When we obey God and walk in His commandments, He helps us succeed in every area of our lives.

Jesus asked for a drink because he wanted to give the Samaritan woman living waters, such that she would not thirst again. Today, Jesus asks for your heart so that you can trust Him and believe in Him. He wants to give you peace in your heart today and eternal life in the life to come. Are you ready and willing to trust the Lord with your heart?

Why not take a moment and say a prayer? Invite Jesus to be Lord and Savior today. Accept His promise of faith and begin a new life in Him. You will experience joy and a peace that is beyond understanding.

23

Now Faith

Hebrews 11:1
Now faith is the substance of things hoped for, the evidence of things
not seen.

Faith is probably one of the most preached topics in Christian circles today. Some see it as this big spiritual gift, reserved for a special few. Is it really?

It will amaze you to know that faith is for everyone and can be exercised in our everyday living. Faith is for you, too. You can have faith. You get many opportunities to apply faith in your everyday life. As we study some of the Bible heroes of faith, I encourage you to identify everyday opportunities to exercise faith in your walk with God.

What is faith? Simply put, faith is trusting God even when we are not sure what the future holds. We need faith for salvation, healing and breakthroughs. We also need faith for obedience and trust that when we do what God's word commands, we can leave the consequences to Him and trust His mighty providence.

How do we gain faith? We gain faith through God's word. God's word has the power to build faith in your heart. *"So, then faith comes by hearing, and hearing by the word of God" (Romans 10:17).*

How much faith do you need? Jesus reminded us that even small faith could do great things. *"If you have faith as a mustard seed, you will say to this mountain, 'Move from here to there,' and it will move" (Matthew 17:20).* Today, how can you exercise your faith?

24

Faith to Obey

Hebrews 11:8
By faith Abraham obeyed.

Our obedience to God shows our faith in Him. Simply put, faith is obedience to God. Every time you see faith in a person's life, you see someone who obeys God regardless of the circumstance.

Oh! That faith will move us as it did for Abraham, who obeyed God and by so doing was called a friend of God.

Noah also showed faith when he built an ark in preparation for a flood that had never occurred before. Imagine being asked to build an ark where there has never been a flood!

"By faith Noah, being divinely warned of things not yet seen...moved with Godly fear..." (Hebrews 11:7)

Sarah also showed her faith when she bore a child after she was past the age of childbearing. She trusted the promise of God. We need faith to believe God for His promises in our lives.

What personal promises has God made to you through His word? Could it be in your family life, in your relationships or in your business endeavour? Could it be in your health, finances, career, academics, marriage, or other areas of your life? Remember, God is able to do great things. He is a miracle-working God. Ask for grace to have faith to obey God and trust in God's promises for you.

25

A GIFT THAT COUNTS

Hebrews 11:4
By faith Abel offered to God a more excellent sacrifice than Cain.

Anyone can give a gift, but it takes faith to give a gift that pleases God. There was a reason Abel's gift was accepted and Cain's rejected. A gift is all the more acceptable when it is given with a happy and cheerful heart. We know from the bible that Cain was an angry person; he must not have been a cheerful giver.

Giving is acceptable to God when you give in obedience and with a cheerful heart. While anyone can give anything at any time, it takes faith to give to God, what He asks you to give and when He asks you to give it.

Abel gave what God wanted, and his gift was accepted. Giving is not always monetary. Sometimes, giving can involve giving of your talent, gift, abilities, time or other resources.

What is God asking you to give today? Could it be to give your heart to Him? Is there some sinful habit that God may be asking you to get rid of? Could God be asking you to give more of your time or to give to the poor and needy? What is God asking you to give to Him?

It takes faith to respond in obedience and give God what He asks of you. Giving is only acceptable to God when done cheerfully. When God asks us to give something, He does so not to burden us, but that He may bless us with exceedingly, abundantly, more.

26

YOUR FUTURE IS
IN HIS HANDS

Hebrews 11:22
By faith Joseph... gave instructions concerning his bones.

Joseph believed in the future God promised the children of Israel. He was thoroughly convinced about God's promise that he gave instructions concerning his bones! Oh, how he did not want even his bones to remain in Egypt when the glorious future of Canaan was promised!

Can you trust God for your future? Can you hold on to His promise for your life, your husband, your wife and your children? Can you trust Him with all that He has planned for your future? Why not stop worrying about your future and learn to trust God more.

Do we, God's children, eagerly look forward to the promised glory, or do we merely strive on this side of eternity with no longing or desire for heaven? Can we, like Joseph, be so determined in our hope for the promise that we will wish for nothing of ours to remain on this side of eternity?

Child of God, may your hope be beyond this earth. May your heart yearn for heaven. May you live with the confidence that God's promises to you will come to pass. Have faith and trust God and, like Joseph, be ready to give instructions that align with your heavenly hope. You can trust God with your future.

27

A Beautiful Child

Hebrews 11:23
By faith Moses, when he was born, was hidden three months by his
parents, because they saw he was a beautiful child.

Pharaoh's decree to kill all the sons born to Hebrew mothers did not prevent Jochebed, Moses' mother from seeing her newborn baby with the eyes of faith. Moses' mother looked at her baby and saw that he was a beautiful child. Through the eyes of faith, she could see that her baby would someday become a great man. How do you see your children? Do you see your children as blessings or as burdens?

You need faith to believe God to save your children. You need faith to trust God for the life of your unborn child. You need faith to persevere in prayer for their wellbeing and success. You need faith to see the beauty in them. You need faith to believe in your children even when others give up on them.

Praying for your children is an excellent way to exercise your faith. Young or old, children will always benefit from a parent's prayer. Even if you don't have children yet, you can pray for the children you will have one day or pray for your nephews and nieces. You can pronounce blessings over your children and pray for their protection. Are you struggling with raising your children? Ask God for the wisdom and grace to raise them according to His will. Are you dealing with a rebellious child? Ask God to help you to see that child through His eyes of love. Trust in God and pray for your child's salvation. It may be tough and long, but never give up hope. May God bless your children.

28

Faith for Tough Times

Hebrews 11:38
They wandered in deserts and mountains, in dens and caves of the earth.

Persecutions, temptations and trials are part of our Christian faith. In life, we will face challenges of different magnitudes and forms in our homes, workplaces, school, business, health, finances and relationships.

To overcome these challenges, we must have faith in God. We must have faith that God will see us through and that He has something better prepared for us. For us to be successful in our journey of faith, we must do two things.

First, we must know what God's word says that we may obey Him. *"Faith comes by hearing and hearing by the word" (Romans 10:17)*. We have determined that obedience to God is the core of our faith, so now we must make an effort to know what the mind of God is. We can know the mind of God through His word.

Second, we must see God's invincible hand in our circumstances. *"For he endured as seeing Him who is invisible" (Hebrews 11:27)*. Regardless of what you may be passing through, I encourage you to see that God is with you, for He promised that He would never leave you or forsake you.

May God grant you the grace to trust Him to see you through tough times. May you see the invisible hand of God in your daily trials and challenges, and may your faith hold firm, knowing that He will be with you and will soon bring you out of your wilderness.

29

THE WORD

John 1:1
In the beginning was the Word, and the Word was with God, and the
Word was God.

Jesus is the word. *"And the Word became flesh and dwelt among us and we*
beheld His glory, the glory as of the only begotten of the Father, full of grace
and truth" (John 1:14).

There is creative power in the word of God. God created the world
by His word. God's children have received the same creative power and
can speak the word of God into any areas of their lives to bring new life,
healing, power and miracles. The word has creative ability; therefore,
speak the word of God over circumstances in your life. *"By faith we un-*
derstand that the worlds were framed by the word of God" (Hebrews 11:3).

The word is a lamp and a light. *"Thy word is a lamp unto my feet and a light*
unto my path" (Psalm 119:105). The word of God gives us direction for life. It
shows us the way to go like a light would light a way ahead for a person. As
a lamp, the word of God lights our path. As light, it causes darkness to give
way. It also reveals any sin within us and causes us to turn away from sin.

The word saves and sanctifies us. The word also heals us and delivers us from bondages. Confess the word of God daily over your life.
Share the word of God with your friends and family as it carries in it the
ability to save, heal, and so much more.

30

A Life Changed

Luke 19:1
Then Jesus entered and passed through Jericho.

Every time Jesus embarks on a journey, someone's life is about to be changed! Every time He passes through, every time He goes to a place, someone's life is about to change.

In Bethany, He raised Lazarus from the dead. He visited Peter, and He healed his sick mother-in-law.

He went through Samaria on His way to Galilee and transformed the life of the Samaritan woman at the well. In Cana of Galilee, He made water turn into wine. He restored a little girl to life. He met ten lepers, and they were healed.

He met the woman with the issue of blood, and she was healed. He gave sight to the blind and caused the lame to walk the deaf to hear, and the dumb to speak. He went about doing good!

How God anointed Jesus of Nazareth with the Holy Spirit and with power, who went about doing good and healing all who were oppressed by the devil, for God was with Him. (Acts 10:38)

Jesus is still in the business of changing lives. In our scripture today, the life of a man named Zacchaeus is changed. As Jesus passes your way today, may your life be transformed!

He can change your life! He will do you good! He has what it takes to transform your life. All you have to do is commit your heart to Him and ask Him to be your Lord and Savior.

3 1

YOUR ASSIGNMENT

Genesis 18:14
And Sarah shall have a son.

Each and every one of us has an assignment from the Lord. We need to understand our assignment from God and fulfill it. Sarah was the one to carry the seed of Abraham.

Whenever God needs to do anything, He needs a seed. But to get the seed, He needs a woman who can carry the seed. Women are special people. Have you ever considered how God delicately created the woman?

God has a unique plan and purpose for all His children, male and female, young and old. What has God created you for? What is your calling and what is your assignment? You may not fully understand it but know that it is not something another can fulfill for you. God is looking to you to walk in your purpose. He is willing to give the grace needed for you to fulfill your destiny. So get ready to step into your calling. No calling is too small or too great.

All tasks are equally important to the Master.

We only need to be willing clay in the hands of the mighty potter and watch as He moulds and makes us into what He originally desired us to be. *"And Sarah shall have a son."* A unique, specific and individual promise, task and assignment which not even Hagar, her maidservant, could fulfill for her.

32

YOU AND YOUR DESCENDANTS

Genesis 9:9
I establish My covenant with you and with your descendants after you.

God is particularly interested in your children. His covenant was made with Noah and his descendants after him. The same was the case for Abraham. God made a covenant with him that extended to his descendants.

As a woman, when you begin to understand your role in the scheme of things, is it any wonder that the enemy is after you and your children?

Satan has used low self-esteem, abuse, rejection, divorce, sin, guilt, sickness, prostitution, dysfunctional relationships, immorality, bereavement, poverty, disappointment and more to hold women captive. Satan knows that if he attacks the woman, then he can destroy the children.

According to the World Food Program USA, about 60% of the world's hungry and poor are women and girls (wfpusa.org). Today the enemy has launched his greatest attack on children and families. He has used drugs, violence, incarceration, alcoholism, rebellion, loss of identity and many other tools to hurt our children. I encourage you to pray for your children.

Arise, cry out in the night, at the beginning of the watches.
Pour out your heart like water before the face of the Lord.
Lift your hands toward Him for the life of your young children,
who faint from hunger at the head of every street.

(Lamentation 2:19)

33

STAND IN THE GAP

Ezekiel 22:30
So I sought for a man among them who would make a wall and
stand in the gap before Me.

God is still looking for those who will stand in the gap of prayer and intercede for their children. We have been given the responsibility to raise godly children. God is counting on you to teach, empower and develop your children for His glory.

God can use any man or woman who is willing. Despite your past or present circumstances, you can become an intercessor and stand in the gap for your family and for your children. You can negotiate the salvation of your family. God needs you. You can stand in the gap for your home. You don't have to be perfect to be used by God in this manner. You only have to be willing to stand in the gap and pray.

God is looking for women who:

- can negotiate like Rahab; have been rejected like Leah.
- are bereaved like Ruth, desperate like Hannah,
- innovative like Jocabed, virtuous like Mary,
- old like Sarah and wise like Abigail;
- have complicated relationships like the Samaritan woman;
- and can pray and fast like Esther.

Start tending to the children God has given you. Start contending for them in prayer. A mother's prayer is a powerful tool that God can use to transform a child's life. Don't give up when it seems like no change is happening. Keep on praying for them and lifting them before God.

34

THE BLESSING

Genesis 12:3
I will bless those who bless you...And in you all the families of the earth shall be blessed.

When God created Adam, He saw that it was not good for Adam to be alone, so He created Eve to be a companion and helper. This was the first family God created. When God saved Noah from the flood, He saved him with his entire family. *"Come into the ark, you and all your household"(Genesis 7:1)*.

Similarly, when God called Abraham, He promised that generations of families would be blessed through him. God loves you and is interested in your family. His blessings are for you and your household. God's blessings are not only for individuals but for their families as well.

God wants you and your family to prosper and to increase in all aspects of your lives. He desires your spiritual and physical well-being. Determine to serve the Lord with your family.

Pray for your spouse, children, parents, siblings and your extended family, too. Make intercession for their salvation, that they may accept Jesus Christ as their Lord and Savior. There is nobody that can pray for your spouse better than you. Cry to God for your children. The blessing of God has been extended to us. Today commit to serve God with your family.

35

THE PAIN OF SEPARATION

Genesis 13: 11
And they separated from each other.

In life, we face different kinds of challenges. Abraham, the father of faith, a friend of God, was not spared from difficulties and challenges. Abraham took his nephew Lot with him on his journey, but a time came when after a misunderstanding between their herdsmen, Lot asked to go his own separate way.

Separation can hurt, especially when we separate from loved ones. Separation can result from a divorce, death or some other reason, and it is never easy. When people leave you, know that God will never leave you. He has promised to always be with you.

Losing my dad when I was a young girl was a very difficult experience for me. I loved my dad and knew that he loved me even more. He raised us in the best way he could, doing his best to make sure the family was well cared for. My dad was my superhero. When he fell sick and later died, I experienced all types of negative emotions. I was angry with myself that I was not able to do something for him. I struggled with a loss of identity and with feelings of shame and inadequacy.

If you find yourself in a similar situation after losing of a loved one or a separation, I want you to know that God loves you, and He will never leave you nor will He forsake you. He will always be by you to hold your hand and lead you on the way.

36

LIFT UP YOUR EYES

Genesis 13:14
Lift your eyes now and look from the place where you are.

It's a new day! Lift up your eyes and see the promises that God has for you! He wants to do something new and special for you. It is time to stop mourning your loss. It is time to wipe your eyes and look up. Look up in hope and see what the Lord will do for you.

God has good plans in store for you. Look up! Do not allow your head to hang low in shame. Look up! There is more that God has in store for you. Stop looking down in shame. Look up! Arise! Get up. Stop hiding. Stop crying. God is about to do something in your life. You cannot see it sitting down. Arise!

And the Lord said to Abram after Lot had separated
from him, "Lift your eyes now and look from the place where
you are, northward, southward, eastward and westward,
for all the land which you see I give to you and your descendants forever."
(Genesis 13:14,15)

Today, I encourage you to look up to the only One who can help you and see the new things that He has in store for you. Your life is not over until

God says so. Move ahead. Let go of the past. Stop mourning for those who have left you. Stop crying over yesterday. Look ahead at tomorrow, for God has yet greater things in store for you. Forget about the things you've been through, for God is bringing you out.

37

THE OPPORTUNITY

Luke 19:6
So he made haste and came down and received Him joyfully.

Zacchaeus had heard that Jesus was coming to the city, and he knew this was an opportunity to see Jesus. He seized the opportunity. Do you recognize opportunity when it comes your way? When life-transforming opportunities come our way, it is important to recognize them and take hold of them.

Some opportunities come when you hear the word of God being preached at your local church, at a retreat or an evangelistic meeting. Indeed, every new day comes with new opportunities that are worth taking hold of.

Opportunity is time-sensitive. It is not guaranteed always to be there. Someone said, "Opportunity knocks but once." The opportunity to encounter Jesus is time-sensitive, and that is why you must take advantage of it when it presents itself. *"Today is the day of Salvation, when you hear his voice do not harden your heart" (Hebrews 3:7).*

Opportunities usually are open to everyone; unfortunately, only a few make good use of them. For your life to appreciate, you must learn to identify opportunities and utilize them wisely.

I had an opportunity to give my life to Christ as a young twelve-year-old, and I took advantage of it. Today, you have an opportunity. Will you take hold of it or will you let it pass you by?

38

NO BARRIERS

Luke 19:3
But could not because of the crowd, for he was of short stature.

There will always be barriers to encountering Jesus.

To have a personal relationship with Jesus, you must face and overcome your barriers. Nothing in life comes easy. Do not give up when you encounter difficulties in your journey to experience Jesus.

Zacchaeus faced two kinds of limitations. First, external limitations *because of the crowd.* These limitations are such things as circumstances you've been through, people, environment, career or finances. What are some of the external challenges that have prevented you from pursuing a closer relationship with Jesus Christ?

Second, Zacchaeus had some personal or internal limitations. *He was very short.* This symbolizes things such as personal challenges, weaknesses, language barriers or feelings of inferiority complex.

You see, whenever God is about to do something in your life, the enemy will push back to stop you.

Are you willing to push past your limitations? You can do it—no more excuses. The time has come for you to leap over the barriers and experience the Lord.

Zacchaeus did not let anything or anyone stop him. He ignored everything and everyone around him, ran ahead, climbed up a sycamore tree, and yes, he caught Jesus' attention, who said to him, *"Zacchaeus make haste and come down, for today I must stay at your house" (Luke 19:5).* You can expect the same answer from the Lord if you will match your faith with purposeful action.

39

THE COMPLAINERS

Luke 19:7
They all complained.

An encounter with Jesus will always attract opposition from some people. Not everyone will support you when you want to turn your life around and become a follower of Jesus Christ. You should not get discouraged when people complain about your love for God.

When God is about to turn your situation around, not everyone will like it. You must be aware that while some family and friends may support you, there may be others who will not support your faith. Do not let their disapproval prevent you from following Jesus. Zacchaeus received Jesus joyfully, and his life was changed forever.

Not only did Zacchaeus experience a genuine encounter with Jesus, but he also overcame hindrances and ignored naysayers. His newfound faith produced sincere repentance in him, and he quickly decided to make restitution for his years of fraudulent activities.

Like Zacchaeus, there must be a real change of heart in us when we follow Jesus Christ. We may not be able to right all the wrongs we did in the past, but there must be a genuine desire and willingness to right wrongs where and when possible.

You can seek counsel from your pastor or trusted brethren in the Lord who can guide you and help you in your new faith. They can also provide guidance for difficult situations or unique circumstances that you face.

40

BEWARE OF COVETOUSNESS

Luke 12:15
And He said to them, "Take heed and beware of covetousness"

In today's world, people are constantly striving to acquire more and more wealth for their future. This excessive greed and quest for more have brought all kinds of evils in society. Cheating, stealing, lying, killing, kidnapping, human trafficking are all products of covetousness. Entire countries have been held to ransom by hoodlums who terrorize and kidnap people.

Individuals, families, corporations and countries have been destroyed by greed, and God's children are warned strongly in today's passage, *"Take heed and beware."* This warning suggests that covetousness can creep into a person's heart if care is not taken. The rich fool did not once acknowledge God's manifold grace in his life; instead, he looked for new ways to store up more riches for himself.

Are you caught in the trap of greed? Do you always crave for that which belongs to another? Hear the Lord's gentle warning, *"Beware of Covetousness."*

God is the source of your success. Without Him, you can do nothing. Recognize and acknowledge His manifold blessings in your life. Always seek out opportunities to support God's work and to give to those who are less privileged. Be thankful for what you do have and ask for the things you desire according to His will. Keep careful watch over your heart lest you be trapped in the crafty web of covetousness.

41

THE EYES OF THE LORD

2 Chronicles 16:9
For the eyes of the Lord run to and fro throughout the whole earth to
show Himself strong on behalf of those whose hearts is loyal to Him.

Friend, God's eyes are on you; therefore, I encourage you to keep your eyes on Him. When trouble comes your way, turn to God with all your heart and seek direction. God is watching to see where you turn to in times of trouble.

God is good and He is faithful. He loves you. In the scripture above, He declares that His eyes run to and fro throughout the whole earth to show Himself strong on behalf of those whose hearts are loyal toward Him. King Asa decided to rely on an enemy king for his safety and deliverance, despite trusting God for deliverance before, and God was unhappy with that. God's rebuke was swift: *"Because you have relied on the king of Syria, and have not relied on the Lord your God, therefore the army of the king of Syria has escaped from your hand." (2 Chronicles 16:7)*

As a child of God, whom will you rely on for help in times of trouble? Who do you seek help from, and from where do you seek help?

May you always go to God for help in prayer. May you take time to seek out His mind concerning your life, your family and everything around you. You serve a faithful God who is always ready and willing to show His mighty power on your behalf. God's eyes are continually watching over you. Are your eyes on the Lord?

42

BEWARE OF EVIL ASSOCIATIONS

2 Chronicles 18:1
Jehoshaphat had riches and honor in abundance, and by marriage he allied himself with Ahab.

Jehoshaphat loved God and showed it, and as a result, he enjoyed God's mighty deliverance when three nations—Moab, Ammon and Mount Seir—came against him. He cried out to God and God helped him. Unfortunately, he did not always exercise sound judgment when it came to his friendships, marriage and business associations.

Jehoshaphat allied himself with Ahab, who was wicked. *"But there was no one like Ahab who sold himself to do wickedness in the sight of the Lord, because Jezebel his wife stirred him up"* (1 Kings 21:25).

Evil associations can bring God's judgment over a person's life. Be careful with your friendships, marriage and even business associations. *"Friendship with the world is enmity with God"* (James 4:4). *"Do not be unequally yoked together with unbelievers"* (2 Corinthians 6:14).

Business partnerships with the wicked can wreck one's hard work. Jehoshaphat's ships were wrecked in Ezion Geber.

*After this, Jehoshaphat king of Judah allied himself with
Ahaziah king of Israel, who acted very wickedly. And he allied
himself with him to make ships to go to Tarshish and they made
the ships in Ezion Geber. But Eliezer the son of Dodavah of Mareshah
prophesied against Jehoshaphat saying, "Because you have allied
yourself with Ahaziah, the Lord has destroyed your works." Then the
ships were wrecked, so that they were not able to go to Tarshish.*

(2 Chronicles 20:35,37)

43

No Disguise

2 Chronicles 18:33
Now a certain man drew a bow at random.

Ahab's cup was full, and God pronounced judgment on him through the Prophet Micaiah. In defiance and disobedience, Ahab disguised himself and went to the battle, saying to himself, *"I will disguise myself and go into battle" (2 Chronicles 18:29).*

Though he tried, Ahab could not disguise himself and avoid facing God's judgment. He planned, schemed, plotted and strategized, yet he could not escape the long hand of judgment for his many sins against God.

Friend, you cannot disguise yourself from the impending judgment that awaits humanity. You cannot hide, plot, plan, scheme or strategize yourself out of it. Today, you can put your trust in Jesus Christ and enjoy the peace that comes from knowing that your sins are forgiven. You can have freedom from sin and the judgment to come. *"For all have sinned and fall short of the glory of God" (Romans 3:23). "And as it is appointed for men to die once, but after this the judgement, so Christ was offered once to bear the sins of many" (Hebrews 9:27).*

In the same battle that killed Ahab, Jehoshaphat cried out to God for help, and God helped him.

"But Jehoshaphat cried out, and the Lord helped him" (2 Chronicles 18:31). May we all cry out to God today for mercy and forgiveness, as no disguise will suffice on that terrible Day of Judgment.

44

DESTINED FOR DELIVERANCE

Exodus: 6:6
I will bring you out from under the burdens of the Egyptians, I will
rescue you.

The children of Israel had been in bondage in Egypt for 430 years. Here
we see a great promise from God to them, *"I will rescue you."*

Dear friend, you are destined for deliverance! God has promised
to deliver you. All you have to do is to accept His promise and commit
your life to Him.

Are you in a dire situation? Are you facing a massive problem? Do
you feel trapped by the struggles within you? I want you to know that
your situation has provided an opportunity for God to show you His
mercy and deliverance. Rejoice, for the promise has come, and you are
destined for deliverance!

Your Deliverance is guaranteed.

"He leads me in the paths of righteousness for His name's sake"
(Psalm 23: 3).

"Like birds flying about, so will the Lord of hosts defend Jerusalem?
Defending, He will also deliver it; passing over, He will preserve it"
(Isaiah 31:5).

The Lord is mighty to deliver. Stop panicking, stop worrying. Cry out to God for mercy. Ask for forgiveness. Commit your life to Jesus Christ and start serving and walking with Him. God has promised to deliver you, and His promises are steadfast. You are destined for deliverance!

45

BE AN EXAMPLE

1 Timothy 4:12
Let no one despise your youth but be an example.

Our faith can be as real and effective in our youthful days as in later years when time and age have taught us some life lessons. We are called to be bold and know that our salvation is genuine and our youth in no way diminishes our faith. Paul admonishes young Timothy to be an example in word. Do you have mastery of the word of God? Do you spend time learning it, loving it, trusting it and obeying its instructions?

Be an example in conduct and behaviour. How, my friend, do you compose and comport yourself? Are you living a careless, carefree and compromising life of worldliness and greed? Be an example in love. Have you learned to show love? Love is the hallmark of our Christian faith. Every virtue, no matter how admirable, is of no eternal value without love. *"Though I speak with the tongues of men and of angels, but have not love, I have become sounding brass or clanging cymbal" (1 Corinthians 13:1).*

Be an example in spirit, in faith and in purity. Let the zeal and passion of your youth reflect in your faith and purity toward the brethren.

Your youth is here. Do not let this season be scorned; instead, cherish, admire and appreciate it. Live your life in full, being careful to be an *example to the believers in word, conduct, love, spirit, faith and purity.*

46

GOD'S PLAN FOR YOUR CHILD

Matthew 18:3
Become as Little Children.

Every time God wants to achieve a unique purpose, He raises a child. In His goal to deliver Jacob and his family through famine, God raised the child Joseph. The child Moses was raised when Israel laboured under bondage in Egypt.

When God wanted to judge the house of Eli, He raised the child, Samuel. When He wanted to deliver Israel from the Philistines, God raised a young lad, David. When God wanted to deliver Mordecai and the Jews in Shushan from an evil Haman, He raised a young girl, Esther. When God wanted a forerunner to prepare the way for the Lord, He raised a child called John the Baptist. When God wanted to send His only Son to deliver the world, He chose a young virgin girl, Mary, to birth our Savior Jesus Christ.

God is still in the business of raising children to fulfill His purposes here on earth. Neglect a child, and you may very well bypass God's miracles and deliverance for you and your family. Did you know that your children are essential to God's plan for your family? Children are a central part of God's plan for the church, society and the world at large. Children are special and uniquely positioned to fulfill destiny when we train them in the way of the Lord.

Today's passage encourages us to become as little children. Let us come to our Heavenly Father with the sincerity and humility of a child and be ready to walk in our God-given assignment as only a child would.

47

No Compromise

Exodus 10:9

We will go with our young and our old; with our sons and our daughters, with our flocks and our herds, we will go.

When asked by Pharaoh, *"Who are the ones that are going?"* Moses did not mince words. He bluntly and directly told Pharaoh who must go on the journey with him. God had commanded Pharaoh to let Israel go from Egypt. Pharaoh did not want to let Israel go. In today's passage, he attempts to negotiate with Moses to allow only the men to go with him to serve God and to keep back the women and children in Egypt.

We sometimes face similar circumstances, where the devil holds back our family members from serving the Lord with us. Satan does not want your family to serve God with you. He attempts to keep family members back from serving God with you. But we must be like the man Moses, who boldly declared, *"We will go with our young and our old; with our sons and our daughters, with our flocks and our herds, we will go...."* *(Exodus 10:9).*

Or we must be like Joshua, who affirmed, *"But as for me and my house, we will serve the Lord"* *(Joshua 24:15).*

Satan continues in his quest to hold back our children. The war against our children is still going on today. It takes the form of abortion, family separation, divorce, child abuse, drugs, alcohol, domestic abuse, child trafficking, child prostitution, child pornography and more. We must continue to stand in the gap for our children and our families and intercede, declaring and decreeing that as for me and my house, we will serve the Lord.

48

In Wisdom, Stature and Favour

Luke 2:52
And Jesus increased in wisdom and stature, and in favor with God and men.

God has a plan for every child. As parents, we will do well to understand God's plan for our children and work accordingly.

Today's passage speaks of four important aspects of your child's growth and development: wisdom—intellectual; stature—physical; favour with God—spiritual growth; favour with man—social growth.

Meeting the intellectual needs of your children is more than just choosing the best schools for them. If our children are to grow in wisdom, the fear of God must be instilled in them from a very young age. Remember, the fear of the Lord is the beginning of wisdom. Being involved in your child's education and participating in their learning are ways of being active in their intellectual development.

"Train up a child in the way he should go and when he is old, he will not depart from it" (Proverbs 22:6).

Increase in stature: providing the necessities of life is part of God's expectation of parents. *"But if anyone does not provide for his own, and especially for those of his household, he has denied the faith and is worse than an unbeliever"* (1Timothy 5:8).

Other needs such as emotional, spiritual and social needs are all part of what every child needs to grow in favour with God and with man. God has a unique plan and purpose for your child. As you partner with Him today, my prayer is that you and your children will be blessed.

49

I HAVE COME DOWN TO DELIVER

Exodus 6:6
I will rescue you from their bondage, and I will redeem you with an outstretched arm.

God is concerned about you. He has promised to rescue you and redeem you with an outstretched arm. Sometimes, problems have a way of making us feel that God has forgotten us, but I have good news for you. God has not forgotten you. He has a plan in place to rescue you.

You may not know the plan, like the children of Israel. However, He saw their pain and predicament, and He set a plan in motion to deliver them. You are not forgotten. Indeed, He has you inscribed on the palms of His mighty hands, so He cannot forget you.

"See, I have inscribed you on the palms of my hands, your walls are continually before me" (Isaiah 49:16).

"Like birds flying about, so will the Lord of hosts defend Jerusalem? Defending, He will also deliver it; passing over, He will preserve it" (Isaiah 31:5).

Lift up your voice to the Lord in prayer. You can be an intercessor for your family. You can stand in the gap and pray for your family. The Hebrew midwives were positioned at their jobs to save the lives of Hebrew babies. Moses was in Pharaoh's palace for a reason; Esther was in the king's palace for a reason. Joseph was both in the prison and the palace for a purpose. You are in your family by design and destiny; therefore, call upon God, who is able to save and deliver. He will deliver you.

50

JOSIAH, A YOUNG KING

2 Kings 22:1
Josiah was eight years old when he began to reign, and he reigned thirty and one years in Jerusalem.

How young is too young to serve God? The perfect time to serve your God is now. Josiah was only eight when he began to reign as king, and he did what was right before the Lord. What can you do for the Lord? The time has come when we must serve God. Instead of piling up excuses, do something now for the kingdom. It will be recorded for you as it was for Josiah.

Four things stand out in his life. First, Josiah did what was right before God. Do we make every effort to please the Lord and to do what is right before Him? Are we comfortable obeying God even when that obedience threatens to bring about challenging circumstances?

Second, Josiah led others toward God. Do you encourage those around you to serve the Lord? Is your zeal for God infectious? Does it stir others to follow Him also?

Third, he made a covenant with God to follow the Lord and to keep His commandments. What commitments have you made to the Lord? Joshua said, *"But as for me and my house, we will serve the Lord" (Joshua 24:15).*

Fourth, Josiah destroyed the worship of Baal, idolatry and witch-craft. What idols are taking God's place in your heart today? Like Josiah, may we pull down every idol and stronghold that hinders us from fully serving and worshiping our God.

5 1

A Father's Love

Luke 15:20
His father saw him and had compassion.

There are many reasons why I love celebrating Father's Day. Fathers are a very important part of our lives and play a distinct and unique role. You can have many friends, mentors or masters, but you only have one father! God is our Heavenly Father.

We have different ways we see God. We may see Him as redeemer, provider, protector and maker. I have come to understand that our knowledge of and relationship with God is distant until we come to know Him personally as our Heavenly Father. This is the most intimate form of relationship with God.

I grew up in a town called Owerri in Imo State, Nigeria, and I was the sixth of eight children. I loved and adored my father. I was his very special daughter. It reminds me of Jacob's love for his son Joseph and how he made him a coat of many colours! The only difference was that my brothers did not hate me! Instead, they would take advantage of my special relationship with Dad and send me to him whenever they needed a special favour from Dad!

Fathers play an important role in the lives of their children. They can inspire and strengthen their children's relationship with God. God knew He could count on Abraham as a father. *"For I have known him, in order that he may command his children and his household after him, that they keep the way of the Lord, to do righteousness and justice"* (Genesis *18:19*).

May the Lord count on you to raise godly children.

52

LESSONS FROM MY FATHER

Genesis 22:7
But Isaac spoke to Abraham his father and said, "My Father!"

From a very young age, Isaac watched his father, Abraham, love and serve God and sacrifice to God Almighty. In today's passage, young Isaac watched Abraham prepare a sacrifice that would forever change their destinies. *"My Father!"* he cried.

I am reminded of seeing my father participate actively in his local church. Whether he was in the city or out in the country, he was always engaged in the local church. He consistently found ways to serve God by serving others. I can truly say that my father inspired my early love for God and the things of God.

There are many lessons my dad taught me, two of which I will share with you today. The first is hard work. I watched my father work very hard to put all eight of his children through university. He showed me that true love provides and cares and is there to guide you every step of the way.

Second, my father taught me never to be afraid to go to him when I made a mistake. Many things terrify children, and one is the fear of falling short of parents' expectations, especially their father. Life is full of ups and downs, and there are times that we will fall short of expectations. Knowing that they are loved can make a difference in the lives of our children.

"My father!" As you call out as Isaac did, may you experience the love, protection, provision, guidance, direction and forgiveness that only your Heavenly Father can give.

53

POSITIONED FOR A PURPOSE

Exodus 1:17
But the midwives feared God and did not do as the king of Egypt
commanded but saved the male children alive.

God positioned Shiphrah and Puah, the Hebrew midwives, for a purpose. Little did they know that they will be instrumental in God's plan
and purpose to deliver the children of Israel from Egypt. Do you know
that God has positioned you in your home, your church and your work-
place for a purpose? There is a role He has for you to play in the deliverance of your family and friends.

The Hebrew midwives were positioned at their job for a purpose.
Moses was positioned in Pharaoh's palace for a purpose. Esther was
placed in the king's palace for a reason. Your position is a potential key
to someone's deliverance.

Whether you are a pastor or a doctor, a nurse or a teacher, a single
mom or a stay-at-home mom, God has positioned you for a season, a
reason, a purpose and a plan. You are a key player in His kingdom business. Jochebed, Moses' mother, was placed there by God. Joseph was
both in the prison and in the palace for a time. The question is, "Where
are you positioned?"

We must stop desiring to take up other people's positions or assignments. Your position is that which God has assigned to you at

this time. It does not matter if it is big or small. In God's overall plan, every one of us counts. The two Hebrew women were just as crucial to God's plan of deliverance as the man Moses, who would lead the mighty exodus.

54

CHOOSING YOUR MARRIAGE PARTNER

Genesis 24:16
Now the young woman was very beautiful to behold.

Choosing your marriage partner is one of the most important decisions you will ever make in your life. To make the right choice of a partner, three things are important. The first is commitment. Abraham was committed to ensuring that his son Isaac married a godly wife. This commitment was shared with his most trusted servant, whose task was to find Isaac a godly wife. We can learn from Abraham's commitment. He knew firsthand the importance of marrying the right person. How important is it for you to find the right partner?

Prayer is the second important thing when choosing a life partner. Like Abraham's servant, we ought to pray and say, *"O Lord God of my master Abraham, please give me success this day" (Genesis 24:12)*. When we pray, we acknowledge God's sovereignty and invite Him into our circumstances to guide and direct us. Every decision in life demands prayer, especially a decision such as marriage, which can impact every aspect of your life, your family and friends.

The third key to choosing a successful partner is a parental blessing. Rebecca was blessed by her family. She did not just get up and elope with Abraham's servant, no. She sought and received blessings from her family before she embarked on her marriage journey. Commitment, prayer and family blessings are three simple keys that can open doors when choosing a life partner. Obeying God in these areas will bring blessings in the marriage.

55

MARRIAGE DECISIONS

Genesis 28:7
And Jacob had obeyed his father and his mother.

Jacob's parents warned him saying, *"You shall not take a wife from the daughters of Canaan" (Genesis 28:6)*. This was because the daughters of Canaan did not serve God, and marrying one of them would lead Jacob away from God.

In today's passage, we see Jacob obeying his parents. Jacob's marriage pleased God and pleased his parents, too. In contrast, Esau's marriage did not please God, and his marriage brought grief to his parents.

> *"When Esau was forty years old, he took as wives Judith the daughter of Beeri the Hittite, and Basemath the daughter of Elon the Hittite. And they were a grief of mind to Isaac and Rebekah"* (Genesis 26:34,35).

What an example for us today? How many marriages would be different if the Holy Spirit were the guide; if prayer, obedience and humility were the order of the day; and if the couple had the blessings of family?

God's word continues to provide us guidance on who to marry. *"Can two walk together, unless they are agreed?" (Amos 3:3)*. We are warned not to become partners with those who reject God. *"Don't become partners with those who reject God. How can you make a partnership out of right and wrong? That's not partnership; that's war. Is light best friends with dark"* (2 *Corinthians 6:14 MSG*)

May we seek God and godly counsel when making decisions, and may we learn to live in obedience to God and His word.

56

BONDING WITH THE BONDWOMAN

1 Corinthians 6:16
Or do you not know that he who is joined to a harlot is one body with
her? "For the two," He says, "shall become one flesh."

God promised Abraham and Sarah a son. When it seemed like God was delaying, Sarah suggested that Abraham have a child with her bondswoman, Hagar. This decision was contrary to God's plan for them.

In life, we often find ourselves in situations where the waiting seems unbearable, and we are tempted to scheme our own blessing in an attempt to do it our way! Like Abraham, we bind ourselves to the *bondwoman* when we fail to wait on God to fulfill His promises to us. When we pursue blessings outside of God's will for our lives, it can lead to various challenges and conflicts in our personal lives. Abraham experienced many conflicts as a result of having a son with Hagar.

Abraham experienced *personal conflict* as tensions soon arose between him and Sarah, his wife, because of Hagar the bondwoman. *"It's all your fault that I am suffering this abuse"* (Genesis 16:5 MSG), Sarah complained bitterly to Abraham.

Emotional conflict was also evident as Sarah dealt harshly with Hagar, causing Hagar to run away. Abraham sent Hagar away with a piece of bread and some water, signifying a *financial conflict* and lack of adequate provision.

When we disobey God in our lives, it can bring about various conflicts in multiple areas of our lives. May God grant us grace to obey Him and wait on Him to fulfill His promises to us.

57

ONE FLESH

Mark 10:8,9
So, then they are no longer two but one flesh: Therefore, what God
has joined together, let not man separate.

God has great plans of blessings for your marriage. He blessed Abraham and promised to channel blessings through him to all other families of the earth. Abraham's blessings are yours to enjoy, too.

Today the family remains the unit of the church and of society. If the family unit crumbles, the church and the society will crumble alike. Unfortunately, the family faces many challenges today, such as divorce, addictions, abuse and separation. The good news is that these challenges are not too big for God.

Let us learn to go to God for the solutions to the troubles we face in the family. He is able to bring hope, peace and love into our hearts and into the hearts of our loved ones. We can do our part to bring about the things that create healing, love, peace, joy and restoration in the family and in all the members.

God has good plans for you, so no matter your situation, you can take your problems to Him in prayer and watch as He begins to piece the broken pieces of your heart back together.

Know that God loves you and His intentions for you are good. If you are blessed with a loving family, give thanks to God. If you face difficulty in your family life, look to God to do that which only He can do. May the Lord bless you and grant you peace, love and joy in your heart and in your family.

58

FINDING YOUR MATE

Proverbs 18:22
He who finds a wife finds a good thing and obtains favor from the
Lord.

When it comes to finding your wife, there are so many factors involved. The good news is that you can partner with God to lead you to the right person.

There are some steps you can take toward finding your marriage partner.

First, develop a close spiritual relationship with God. Having a personal relationship with Jesus continues to be a priority if you are looking for spiritual guidance to finding a marriage partner. You must trust that God wants your ultimate good. When you develop a close relationship with God, you will begin to understand how He speaks to you.

Second, cultivate the art of paying attention to spiritual things and hearing God's gentle leading, prompting and direction for your life.

Third, learn to make whatever necessary changes or adjustments that you sense God could be leading you to make, even if it seems small, insignificant or unnecessary.

God wants you to find your marriage partner. He also wants you to be happy, busy and productive while you wait. As you lean in to have a closer relationship with God, listen in for His guidance, leading and direction and put into practice the changes He wants you to make in your life or do the things He asks you to do. He will surely fulfill your heart's desires, and you will *"obtain favor from the Lord."*

59

KEEPING YOUR HEART

Proverbs 4:23
Keep your heart with all diligence, for out of it spring the issues of life.

It is vital to keep your heart pure because from your heart come the issues of life. Your heart is the center of your being. We love God from our hearts, we commune with Him from our hearts, God searches our hearts, and we believe in God from our hearts. It is essential that we guard our hearts against defilement through emotional trauma, sin, evil, lies, condemnation, doubt, pride, unforgiveness, grief and other things.

> *"My heart is in turmoil and cannot rest; days of affliction confront me" (Job 30: 27).*

Another issue we must guard our hearts against is sin. *"Your word have I hidden in my heart that I may not sin against you" (Psalm 119:11).* Constant study of God's word builds up your spirit, giving you grace and strength to overcome sin and temptation.

We guard our hearts when we refuse to engage in sinful works of the flesh.

> *"Now the works of the flesh are evident, which are: adultery, fornication, uncleanness, lewdness, idolatry, sorcery, hatred, contentions,*

jealousies, outbursts of wrath, selfish ambitions, dissensions, heresies,
envy, murders, drunkenness, revelries and the like" (Galatians 5:21)

Guarding our hearts is not something we can do alone. We are to rely on God to grant us the grace to dwell on His word while avoiding the things that defile our hearts. It is a good time to start afresh with a new and total dependence on God.

60

YOUR BODY, GOD'S TEMPLE

1 Corinthians 6:19
Do you not know that your body is the temple of the Holy Spirit who
dwells in you, whom you have from God, and you are not your own?

God has purchased us with a price, and we belong to Him. The Holy Spirit dwells in us! What a privilege that our bodies can be the dwelling place for the Holy Spirit.

Have you ever had a very special guest who was coming to stay in your home for a few days? How did you prepare your home for your special guest? I'll tell you how I'll keep mine. I'll clean my entire house from top to bottom. I will ensure I have everything my guest will need to be comfortable in my home.

In today's passage, it is not just any regular guest in our homes; it is the Holy Spirit who wants to dwell with us and in us. Realizing how awesome this special guest is, we ought to do everything to ensure our bodies are conducive for Him. We need to allow God to clean us up and help us to maintain our *temple* as a constant, welcome dwelling for Him.

When we engage in premarital sex, we dishonour our bodies, forgetting that the Holy Spirit of God is inside of us.

"Flee sexual immorality, every sin that a man does is outside the body, but he who commits sexual immorality sins against his own body" (I Corinthians 6:18).

In His infinite wisdom, God knows all the dangers posed by this deadly trap and urges His children everywhere to avoid it.

61

LUST'S DESTRUCTIVE POWER

Proverbs 6:26
For by means of a harlot a man is reduced to a crust of bread.

Lust is sinful and destructive and can hinder us from being all that God wants us to be. The lives of many individuals and families have been ruined in many ways by the effects of lust.

Lust originates in the heart and thereby appears very harmless. As it seems harmless, usually nothing is done to control it, thereby leaving it to fester and strengthen its monstrous grip on a person's life. Lust often leads to other harmful habits such as pornography and sexual immorality.

Though lust appears innocent, the effects show that it is not. It is a deadly trap, prepared by the enemy to ambush even the best of God's children unawares.

Lust has left many casualties in its wake. It has destroyed the lives of many people. *"Whoever commits adultery with a woman lacks understanding; He who does so destroys his own soul. Wounds and dishonor he will get, and his reproach will not be wiped away"* (Proverbs 6:32,33).

One sure way to protect your heart from lust is to cleanse your mind with the word of God daily. *"How can a young man cleanse his way? By taking heed according to your word"* (Psalm 119:9).

"That they may keep you from the immoral woman, from the se-ductress who flatters with her words. For she has cast down many wounded, all who were slain by her were strong men" *(Proverbs 7:5,26).*

May the Lord deliver you from every trap of the enemy, and may you continually overcome.

62

Raising Lazarus

John 11:1
Now a certain man was sick, Lazarus of Bethany.

Have you ever needed a miracle? Have you needed God to do something out of the ordinary for you? Lazarus was sick, and immediately the sisters sent for Jesus. *"Lord, behold, he whom You love is sick."* The miracle in Bethany is similar to the miracle Jesus wants to perform in your life today.

My life has been full of miracles from the Lord. First, when I was a toddler, my mum recounts that I had a hot water accident. I had climbed up a kitchen stool to look up the kitchen counter to watch my sister cook. Needless to say, I suffered first-degree burns all over my body. I was then rushed to the University Medical Center close to the house, by Zik's drive, in Enugu, Nigeria. The doctors battled to save my life. They were certain I had become blind as my eyes could not open for seven days! Nobody believed that I would see again, but God worked a miracle!

A second incident occurred when I was one year old. There was a diarrhea outbreak at the University of Nigeria campus which killed many babies. The diarrhea was so severe that all efforts to contain it at the University Medical Center were to no avail. The situation was desperate, and again the doctors tried to save my life and could not locate any vein in my tiny body. My mum recounts that she thought all hope was lost, but once again, God showed up.

God is still in the business of performing miracles. He is able and also willing to intervene in your life. I invite you to call on Jesus as Mary and Martha did, and He will show up and do a miracle for you.

63

A Spirit of Infirmity

Luke 13:11
There was a woman who had a spirit of infirmity.

A spirit of infirmity had crippled this poor woman so much that she was bent over and could not lift herself up. For eighteen good years, her body was wrecked by this awful spirit of infirmity. But upon encountering Jesus, her life was changed for good, forever. What an awesome God we serve!

In life, we sometimes feel like this woman—sick, bent over, burdened and, worse still, unable to help ourselves. It could be physical, mental or emotional sickness. What has bowed you together? What has crippled you? What is hindering you from becoming everything that God designed for you to become?

Sin, sickness, disease, poverty, worry, depression, guilt and anxiety are all cripplers. Perhaps you have tried but cannot lift yourself up. You try to be happy, but before long, depression finds its way back into your heart. You try to forgive and move forward with your life, but the pain still hurts inside of your heart. You feel paralyzed, crippled and completely boxed in.

The Lord wants to heal you. Today, Jesus is calling out to you. He is reaching out to you because He created you for a purpose and He wants you to fulfill the purpose for which He created you. God wants to turn your circumstances around. He is willing and ready to help you. He is calling out to you this day with a voice of faith and declaring boldly over you as One who has been given all authority in heaven, on earth and beneath the earth. Thus, says the Lord to you, *"Woman, you are loosed from your infirmity" (Luke 13:12).*

64

TEN LEPERS

Luke 17:12
He entered a certain village, there met Him ten men who were lepers,
who stood afar off.

Jesus was passing through Samaria and Galilee on his way to Jerusalem when He met ten men who were lepers and who stood afar off. Leprosy was a disease that not only plagued the person physically but also alienated him or her from the service and worship of God. Lepers could not go into the temple. They were outcasts and considered to be unclean. A certain area was designated for them to stay, and they could not mingle freely with others. Not only were they sick in body, but they also faced discrimination, and as a result, they *"stood afar off."*

When Jesus healed the ten lepers, He not only took away their sickness, but He also took away their reproach, their separation from God, their shame, their lowly status, and He made them clean!

This is very similar to what Jesus has done for us. In dying on the cross for us, He took away our sin and separation from God. He forgave us, cleansed us, and gave us free access to worship our God. Jesus has paid the full price for your salvation. Have you accepted Jesus into your life as your Lord and Savior?

"'Go, show yourselves to the priest,' Jesus said to the ten lepers. And so, it was, that as they went, they were cleansed" (Luke 17:14). Your miracle is awaiting your obedience. Hear the command of the Lord to you today, and obey what the Lord has commanded.

65

YOUR DRY BONES
SHALL LIVE AGAIN

Ezekiel 37:3
Son of man, can these bones live?

God brought Ezekiel to a valley full of dry bones to show him something significant. Ezekiel noticed three striking things about the bones. First, they were very many of these bones. Bones represent spiritual death or dead areas of our physical lives. These circumstances were enormous. Second, the bones were left in an open valley. You see, these had actually been buried, but they had become exposed for anybody to see over time. Your problems—both spiritual and physical—may have been hidden from those around you before, but now it seems that Satan has even gone the extra mile to expose you in order to put you to shame. Third, the bones were very dry. The spiritual state of the people was very deplorable. It was deemed hopeless.

Then the Lord asks the question, "Son of man, *can these bones live?*" I have come to understand that when God asks you a question, He is not seeking out information; He is using the question to stir up faith in your heart. Jesus did the same thing. He asked people lots of questions. *Jesus asked the blind man, "Do you believe that I am able to do this?"* (Matthew 9:27).

What question is the Lord asking you today? Questions provide an opportunity to expose the thoughts of the heart. Every question is an opportunity to express fear or declare faith. Questions reveal the thought of a man's heart. What is God's question to you today? How will you respond? As for Ezekiel, he responded, *"O Lord God, you know."*

66

Prophesy to Your Problems

Ezekiel 37:4
Prophesy to these bones, and say to them, "O dry bones, hear the word of the LORD!"

Hear a command from the Lord, dear friend, prophesy to your *dry bones* and tell them to hear the word of the Lord. What an amazing invitation from God! You have been given a task so important, so direct to accomplish. He commands you not to dwell on the problem nor to meditate upon the problem, but to speak to the problem. Often, we rather cry, moan, and grow anxious because of the *valley of dry bones* all around us. The insurmountable problems of life are not impossible with God, for with God all things are possible.

> *"Say to them," commands the Lord to Ezekiel. But what was Ezekiel to say to the dry bones? Was he to analyze and proffer some possible solutions? Was he to think of reasons why it would be impossible for life to come upon the dry bones? No. Rather the command was unambiguous. It was clear as day and it said, "Prophesy to these bones and say to them, 'O dry bones, hear the word of the Lord! Thus, says the Lord God to these bones...'" (Ezekiel 37:4, 5).*

God commanded Ezekiel to speak *His word* to the dry bones. Your problems are not waiting for your analysis; they are waiting for a word from the Lord!

God's word is stronger than any human wisdom.

> *"Surely, I will cause breath to enter into you, and you shall live. I will put sinews on you and bring flesh upon you, cover you with skin and put breath in you; and you shall live. Then you shall know that I am the Lord" (Ezekiel 37:5, 6).*

Oh, my soul, hear the word of the Lord! Speak the word of the Lord and nothing but the word! Amen!

67

FINDING YOUR REST

Mark 6:31
Come aside by yourselves to a deserted place and rest a while.

Beloved, rest is good for you. In today's passage, the apostles had been so busy ministering to the people, that they did not find time to eat. Jesus then encouraged them to take some time away from the crowd and get some much-needed rest. *"And He said to them, 'Come aside by yourselves to a deserted place and rest a while.' For there were many coming and going, and they did not even have time to eat. So they departed to a deserted place in the boat by themselves"* (Mark 6:31, 32).

It is good to work hard. It is also good to know when to take regular rests to avoid being burned out.

Rest enables you to recharge and be more effective in what you do for the Lord. Finding time to spend alone with God in His word and prayer is key to having a successful life and ministry. If we are constantly on the go and never find time to rest, we will find ourselves in situations where we are overwhelmed, depressed, stressed out and anxious.

We will become easily irritable and upset if we are constantly busy and do not take a break. If we do not take care, our spiritual, mental, emotional and physical health will all be at risk when we refuse to rest up.

Jesus found time to spend alone in prayer. He also encouraged His apostles to take rest. Permit yourself to rest. When you regularly rest you will always be able to do more work for the Lord.

68

SERVING GOD IN THE FACE OF PROBLEMS

Luke 1:11
Then an angel of the Lord appeared to him, standing on the right side of the altar.

Zacharias and Elizabeth were both serving God, yet they had a need in their lives. *"So it was, that while he was serving as priest before God in the order of his division" (Luke 1:8)*. They were faithful, but they had a problem; they had no child. Problems in life are not an indication that we are out of favour with God. You can love God and serve God faithfully and yet have problems in your life. We can see problems as an opportunity for God to do the impossible in our lives.

There is something about serving God in the face of challenges. Never let your problems stop you from serving God. Zacharias had a challenge, but he continued to serve God. He was well advanced in age, but he continued to serve God. His wife was barren, but he continued to serve God. How about you? Are you serving God despite your problem?

Are you continuing to serve God in the face of financial difficulty, sickness, loss of a loved one, joblessness, childlessness, addictions or other problems? When you serve God despite your problem, He sends an angel. Yes, His eyes are on you. He will send you help. Don't give up.

Hold on! Hang in there. Keep serving God and keep trusting Him. He sees you and hears your prayer. Soon an angel will be dispatched to you with a heavenly message as was with Zacharias. *"Do not be afraid, Zacharias, for your prayer is heard" (Luke 1:13)*

May the Lord, who sees you and hears you, answer you speedily.

69

YES, IT'S POSSIBLE

Luke 1:37
For with God nothing will be impossible.

Today, I bring you a message of gladness and hope. God is pouring out blessings upon His people, and you are one of them. Prepare to receive that which God has for you. Be ready to see God do the impossible in your life.

> *"Now indeed Elizabeth your relative has also conceived a son in her old age, and this is now the sixth month for her who was called barren. For with God nothing will be impossible" (Luke 1:36, 37).*

The angel testifies to Mary of God's goodness toward her relative, Elizabeth, to stir up her faith and cause her to believe what God is about to do through her. God is still in the business of blessing lives and giving miracles. He has enough blessings for everyone! It is a season of blessing. God has dispatched His angels to bring the good news of answered prayers to you.

He has enough blessings for all His children. You never have to be jealous of the blessings of other people. Instead, learn to rejoice with others when they rejoice and keep trusting God for your own special blessing. This is the season for testimonies of what God has done.

Share what God has done for you with your family and friends to encourage them to trust God for their own blessings, too. The angel told Mary about Elizabeth's miracle. *"Now indeed, Elizabeth your relative has conceived a son in her old age; and this is now the sixth month for her who was called barren. For with God nothing will be impossible" (Luke 1:36, 37).*

70

Touching Jesus

Luke 8:44
Came from behind and touched the border of His garment. And
immediately her flow of bleed stopped.

Throughout the ministry of Jesus, we see Him touching people to minister healing and deliverance. Today, let us see the ministry of Jesus from another angle, *us touching Jesus*. Something happens when we make contact with Jesus. How do we touch the Master, and what happens when we touch Him?

We need not touch Jesus physically to experience the miraculous power. Neither do we need to touch His picture or His statue. We don't touch Jesus through our self-righteousness, nor do we need to visit a shrine. The question then is, "How do we touch Jesus?"

"Now a woman, having a flow of blood for twelve years, who had spent all her livelihood on physicians and could not be healed by any, came from behind and touched the border of His garment. And immediately her flow of blood stopped" (Luke 8: 43,44).

First, she came from behind a crowd thronging Jesus. Have you tried getting someone's attention in a crowd? She had to press through the crowd to reach her hand close enough to *"touch the border of His garment."* Second, she had a disease for twelve long years, was drained of her livelihood, was desperate and was out of options. Third, her touch was no ordinary touch. It was a touch of faith. Her faith overcame every kind of hindrance that she came across. A kind of faith that is not fearful but instead shuns every scorn and intimidation. *"Daughter, be of good cheer; your faith has made you well. Go in peace." (Luke 8:48).*

Today, reach out and touch Jesus in faith.

71

You, Family, Ministry and Career

Judges 4:4
Now Deborah, a prophetess, the wife of Lapidoth, was judging Israel at that time.

It can be challenging to juggle many titles and wear so many hats at the same time. When God gives a task, He also gives the grace to carry out the assignment He has given. We are all different, and our callings vary. There is no small assignment so long as you remain faithful and do the Lord's will.

Like Deborah, God sometimes calls us to multiple assignments. A prophetess, a wife, a mother and a judge in Israel! Let's not try to do it all by ourselves; rather, let us rely on the grace that He provides to make a difference in our home, church, community and the marketplace. God can use any woman who is willing. God continues to use women from all walks of life. Women who can judge like Deborah or can negotiate like Rehab. Women who have been rejected like Leah, hurt like Tamar or bereaved like Ruth. Women like Hannah, who prayed for a child, or like Jocabed, who found ingenious ways to save hers. Women who are virtuous like Mary, old like Sarah, wise like Abigail, or can pray and fast like Esther.

Women who have complicated relationships like the Samaritan woman or been caught in adultery. Women from who Jesus cast out demons, like Mary Magdalene, or were healed of their diseases. Women who made meals for Jesus or sat by His feet to learn. Women who supplied for His ministry or those who gave their precious alabaster flask with indescribable gratitude.

72

THE TEMPTATIONS OF JESUS

Matthew 4:3
If You are the Son of God, command that these stones become bread.

Jesus was tempted in every way like we are today. How did He pull off such a victory against the devil? Every day we face diverse challenges and temptations that cause us to disobey God. Sometimes these temptations are too subtle to identify and very difficult to resist.

Temptation can occur at any time, including after great spiritual experiences. Jesus had just had a baptism where God declared His Sonship with a voice from heaven. Temptations can sometimes last for a long time or a short time. Satan is the tempter, for God cannot be tempted with evil. Satan tempts us by drawing us or enticing us with our own lusts or desires (James 1:14).

The temptation here was for Jesus to use his power and privilege as the Son of God for His own advantage. To take that which God had not given Him at that time. In what ways are we tempted to use our position to our advantage? There are so many temporary things that we need and pursue at the expense of eternal life. When we are tempted to fulfill our desires of the flesh in disobedience to the word of God, we must remember that disobedience to God has eternal consequences.

Jesus overcame so that you and I can overcome also. God promised to give us sufficient grace to overcome every temptation. May we humbly rely on His grace to overcome every temptation that comes our way.

73

Preparing for the Bridegroom

Matthew 25:4
But the wise took oil in their vessels with their lamps.

The Church awaits the return of her Bridegroom. However, tired of waiting, many have fallen off by the wayside of life, lured by the snares of the world. Today, I encourage you to hold on and be ready as we wait for the return of our Lord.

There were ten virgins, and they all had their lamps. This shows all ten of them intended to see the Bridegroom. They were not merely pretending to be interested; they actually desired to see Him. They all went to meet the Bridegroom. They were not idle; they were serving in the house, perhaps singing in the choir, ushering, teaching in the nursery. They all went to meet the Bridegroom; however, five were prepared and five were not.

The difference was in the oil. The foolish took no oil, but the wise did. The oil represents the Spirit of God.

"You were sealed by the Spirit..." (Ephesians 1:13).

Some things about oil: Oil is a lubricant; oil cleans, inhibits corrosion and cools engines. Oil is also a preservative. When used in cooking, good oil adds taste to the food. Oil needs to be renewed every once in a while. You have to live in the Spirit continuously. You cannot depend on the life you lived many years ago or the preparation you made a while back. Instead, you have to equip yourself daily and be ready to meet your Lord Jesus.

Don't leave yourself unprepared; instead, have constant communion with the Holy Spirit of God that you may be ready when the trumpet sounds.

74

THE BORROWED AXE

2 Kings 6:5
And he cried out and said, "Alas, master! For it was borrowed."

When we face various kinds of challenges, we are sometimes tempted to hide these difficulties from others out of shame and pride.

There seems to be a culture that suggests that your life should be problem-free if God is with you.

God did not promise us a life free of challenges; rather He promised to always be with us and help us overcome the challenges we face. We should not pretend that all is well when we are hurting inside. God wants us to cry out to Him for help when we need it, and He will always come to our rescue.

In today's passage, the sons of the prophets, under Elisha's tutelage, were working on a project when they encountered a problem. A borrowed axe being used by one of them fell into the water, creating a major hold-up in the project and a potential reputational and financial burden for the sons of the prophets. *"But as one was cutting down a tree, the iron ax head fell into the water; and he cried out and said, 'Alas, master! For it was borrowed'"* (2 Kings 6:5).

Problems can come your way even when you are doing the very thing God wants you to do. Problems are not a sign that one is out of favour with God; instead, they provide an opportunity for God to manifest His power in our lives. Like the sons of the prophets, let us learn to cry out to God for help when we face difficulties, and a miracle will be worked to make our axe head float again.

75

GO THE DISTANCE

John 19:25
Now there stood by the cross of Jesus His mother, and His mother's sister, Mary the wife of Clopas, and Mary Magdalene.

Throughout the earthly ministry of Jesus, crowds followed him. However, not many were able to follow Him through the most challenging times of His earthy ministry. From the start of His arrest, trial, crucifixion, death and resurrection, many people followed Him, but very few went the distance and followed Him until the end. It was a difficult time for His mother, disciples, friends and some exceptional women who followed Him till the end.

Today, be encouraged by the tenacity of these women who went the distance with Jesus. Often, we are tempted to give up on following Jesus, to give up on our faith, children, marriage, family or church family. Many have been discouraged from following after the Lord, but I have good news for you. If you do not quit, if you will go the distance, if you will stay with the Lord, if you will seek Him early, *the stone will be rolled away. (Luke 24:2)*

These women, many of whom ministered to Jesus from their resources, were ordinary women from various walks of life. Some were married, some were mothers and some entrepreneurs. They served and ministered to Jesus with their resources. Do you have any excuse for not serving God? Remember, it is not how you start but how you finish. The crowd returned from following Jesus, but a few continued to follow Him to the end. Let us be one of those.

76

LET THERE BE MORE DEBORAHS

Judges 4:14
Then Deborah said to Barak, "Up! For this is the day in which the Lord delivered Sisera into your hand."

Let there be more Deborahs. That is definitely a cry from the heart of God. Whenever God is about to do something, He places men and women in strategic positions to use them to achieve His purpose. God is moved by those who allow themselves to be used by Him.

You have been chosen for a time like this. Every one of us has a present assignment from the Lord. We need to understand our assignment from God and fulfill it now while there is time. Deborah was a prophetess, a wife and a judge. First, as a prophetess, this signifies our relationship with God. Our relationship with God comes first and foremost before any other earthly relationship. Second, she was described as a wife; our earthly relationship is unique and very important to God. Our position and duty in the family are critical to God's plan and purpose.

Third, she was described as a judge in Israel. Our careers follow after our spiritual and family duties. Our many tasks and callings should work hand in hand. No one aspect should obscure the other. God acknowledges these unique ministries and wishes for us to bring them in harmony. You should not have to choose between ministry or family.

God wants to use you as you are—a mother, a wife, a father, a grandmother, single, married or widowed. In whatever situation you find yourself, the Lord can use you. Let us rise up and motivate those around us.

77

LETTERS FROM THE LORD

Revelation 3:22
Hear what the Spirit says to the churches.

We all love to get emails, messages and notifications. The brief and somewhat noisy beep of your phone often interrupts your business and alerts you to a new message. Not all notifications, alerts, messages or mails are of the same importance. We like to get emails from people we like. No one likes junk mail.

How will you love to get a letter from the Lord? In the book of Revelations, we are introduced to letters from the Lord to the seven churches, and in today's scripture verse, we are encouraged to hear what the Spirit has to say to the churches. The Lord is constantly sending us messages through His word. Even now, He is writing you a very real and personal letter.

In His letter to the Philadelphian church He says,

"And to the angel of the Church in Philadelphia write, 'these things says He who is Holy, He who is true, "He who has the key of David, He who opens, and no one shuts, and shuts and no one opens"
(Revelation 3:7)

In His letter to the church in Philadelphia, much effort is put into describing the Lord. There is something to be said about knowing the Lord deeper than most people do, knowing the holiness and the omnipotence of our Lord. Let us draw closer to experience the holiness of our Lord and His mighty power. Let us go beyond mere head knowledge and stand in awe of our Holy Savior, the One who holds the key to unlock every closed door and show us great and mighty things that we did not know.

78

LIVING LIFE STRESS-FREE

Luke 10:40
But Martha was distracted with much serving.

Most women can identify with Martha. We know the constant craving to run a clean home. Do you remember those school mornings when your little one could not find his pair of shoes or socks? Do you remember running errands, fixing dinner, doing dishes, laundry and everything in between?

The need to fix, clean and organize can wear you out. The Lord wants you to learn the key to living a stress-free life. It is easy to find yourself constantly under pressure and be worn out with things that need your attention. Complaining, irritability and fault-finding become our companions when we are tired.

Martha found herself overwhelmed with housework that she came to Jesus and complained about her sister, Mary. *"Lord, do You not care that my sister has left me to serve alone? Therefore, tell her to help me." (Luke 10:40)*

Try as she may, Martha could not deceive the Lord. Jesus knew that the real problem was not her sister, Mary; her problem was that she was distracted from the Lord.

We can find our rest in the Lord if we spend quality time with the Lord in our daily devotions. We can be empowered, encouraged, inspired and strengthened for all the tasks we have to do. When we place the tasks ahead and allow ourselves to be consumed by all the things we have to do, we become tired and worn out, and like Martha, we blame family and friends. Today, pause and strengthen yourself in the Lord. His rest will always take away your stress.

79

First Love

Revelation 2:4
You have left your first love.

There is something about first love. It is full of fervor, passion, zeal and intensity. It draws two lovers closer to each other and everything else appears insignificant when they are in each other's embrace. Similarly, when we first fall in love with the Lord, we are passionate about spending time with Him and doing the things that bring Him joy and glory.

How is your love toward the Lord today? Are you still as passionate and zealous for Him as you once were? Has your love grown from strength to strength, or has your love gone cold? Do you feel the passion of your first love, or have you lost your first love?

Have possessions, people, places, power, positions or problems taken that which once belonged to the Lord? Has the flame of your love for Christ ebbed because of friendship with the world?

Today, the Lord is calling us back to Himself. He does not leave us wondering what we must do to be restored. He urges us, *"Remember therefore from where you have fallen; repent and do the first works, or else I will come to you quickly and remove your lampstand from its place – unless you repent"* (Revelations 2:5).

"Dear Lord, help us to love you like we once did. Forgive us our sins and renew your love deep inside our hearts. Help us to love you more than we ever did at first. May your love draw us closer to you."

8 0

MIRACLES

Ephesians 3:20
Now to Him who is able to do exceedingly abundantly above all that
we ask or think, according to the power that works in us.

God desires to do a miracle for all His children. Each day of our lives
gives God an opportunity to do a miracle in our lives. Faith is essential to
your miracle; prayer is essential to your miracle. There is a third factor
necessary for the miraculous power to operate in your life, obedience.

When Elijah proclaimed a drought by the word of the Lord, and
there was no rain for three years in Israel, God made a way to ensure
Elijah was fed. Elijah obeyed and followed God's leading and direction, and he drank by the Brook Cherith. Later, as he continued to
follow God's direction, *"The ravens brought him bread and meat in the*
morning and bread and meat in the evening; and he drank from the brook."
(1 Kings 17:6)

When the brook dried up, God had another plan, all carefully laid
out. All Elijah had to do was obey the word of the Lord, and God would
take care of him. *"Arise, go to Zarephath, which belongs to Sidon, and*
dwell there. See, I have commanded a widow there to provide for you."
(1 Kings 17:9).

Our obedience is the powerful key that unlocks God's blessings in
our lives. God did not only plan for Elijah's provision, He also planned

for the widow and her house. For as it was with Elijah, she also discovered that if she would only believe and obey the Lord, the Lord will do the impossible *"So she went away and did according to word of Elijah; and she and he and her household ate for many days"* (1 Kings 17:15).

81

Praising Your Way Out with Thanksgiving

Luke 17:18
Were there not any found who returned to give glory to God?

We should always be thankful to God for the great things He does in our lives. God is always ready to bless us despite our shortcomings. He will bypass rules and make exceptions to bless us though we may be undeserving. Think of all the blessings God has brought your way. Remember when you did not qualify for that job, but you got hired anyway. Remember when everyone gave up on you, but God gave you another opportunity? It didn't matter that your loved ones deserted you. It didn't matter that you couldn't lift your face out of guilt and shame. It didn't matter that you were not deserving, God blessed you anyway. Do you remember where you were and what you were doing when the Lord found you?

For the lepers that encountered Jesus in today's bible verse, a word from the Lord was all they needed to receive their healing from leprosy. Notice that their healing only took place when they obeyed the Lord's command to them. Some people want to see the miracle before they praise God. The lepers were restored as they obeyed the Lord. Don't wait on your praise to God. Don't delay in obeying the Lord. Don't hesitate in His service, for as you do so, your miracle will take place.

"And one of them when he saw that he was healed, returned and with a loud voice glorified God, and fell down on his face, at His feet, giving Him thanks" (Luke 17:15,16)

Today, you have an opportunity to glorify God. I encourage you to rejoice and be glad for the Lord is good and His mercies endure forever. Stop complaining; instead, start praising. Your praise has the potential to unlock the door to your healing and your miracle. Let us be counted among those who return to give God praise.

82

THE HEART OF
TRUE WORSHIP

Malachi 1:2
Yet you say, "In what way have You loved us?"

When God used the Prophet Malachi to confront the children of Israel about their sinful life and poor worship, instead of repenting and seeking forgiveness, they posed arrogant questions to God. When God confronts us with sin, let us quickly humble ourselves and repent. First, they questioned God's love. *"In what way have you loved us?" (Malachi 1:2)*, they asked. Questioning God's love is an indicator of a poor state of a person's heart or worship to God. When we say things like "If God loves me, why did He let this happen?" we question God's love for us. God is always faithful and can never be unfaithful.

"In what way shall we return?" (Malachi 3:7). Here, they questioned their sinful backsliding. There are people who, when confronted with sin, feign ignorance. You cannot overcome something you have not recognized. When confronted by God's word about sin in our lives, it is wise for us to go before God in humility to ask for forgiveness. *"I acknowledged my sin to You, and my iniquity I have not hidden. I said, 'I will confess my transgressions to the Lord' and You forgave the iniquity of my sin" (Psalm 32:5)*

"In what way have we robbed you?" *(Malachi 3:8)*. When confronted about the poor sacrifices they brought to God, the children of Israel asked how they had robbed God. When we do not see God as our ultimate provider, we fail to understand that all we possess comes from the Lord. A poor attitude to giving indicates a poor heart of worship.

"In what way have we spoken against you?" *(Malachi 3:13)*. Do we speak against God, His servants, His church or His people? Let us not be those who talk about others behind their back. As you reflect on today's bible verse, May the Lord create a new heart of worship in you.

83

REMEMBERING THE LORD'S GOODNESS

2 Samuel 7:8
I took you from the sheepfold, from following the sheep, to be ruler over My people, over Israel.

God remembers all He has done for you; do you?

Today we want to take some time and remember God's goodness. I challenge you to take some time and remember the goodness of God in your life and in that of your family, like David did. *"For the Lord is good and His mercies endure forever" (Psalm 100:5).*

David was a man who remembered God's goodness. Every time he faced a challenge, he recalled God's goodness to him. Do you remember God's goodness when you face challenges? Remembering will help you trust God to deliver you in tough times.

David could put his faith firmly in God when he faced Goliath because he remembered how God had delivered him before. *"The Lord who delivered me from the paw of the lion ...He will deliver me from the hand of this Philistine" (1 Samuel 17:37).*

In good times as well, David never forgot God's goodness to him. In one of such moments, he thought of building God a house. This act caused God to send the Prophet Nathan to tell David of the great things God would do for him and his family in the years to come.

Remembering God's goodness will cause you always to be thankful. It will also inspire you to serve God more faithfully. God remembers how far He has brought you; do you remember? Let us take some time today to remember and be thankful.

84

HER ALABASTER FLASK

Mark 14:3
A woman came having an alabaster flask of very costly oil of spikenard.

Jesus' ministry was marked with multiple healings and deliverances in the lives of ordinary people. He saved, healed, delivered and provided for men, women, children, lepers, the sick and those possessed by demons. He healed the rich and the poor alike.

In today's scripture, Jesus sat at the table of Simon the leper. Simon was a leper, yet Jesus was seated at a table with him. Has it ever occurred to you that Jesus broke down many barriers just to meet us where we were? As Jesus sat at Simon's house, a woman came, having something of great value. The Bible describes it as an alabaster flask of very costly oil of spikenard. It was a very special and expensive perfume. She carried this very special alabaster flask containing costly oil and perfumes, and she broke it and poured it out on Jesus' head.

What is in your precious alabaster flask? What would you give to show your love to Jesus? What is the precious oil that you are going to bring to Jesus? Could it be you? Could it be your love and devotion? Could it be your praise? What is that priceless gift that you can bring your Lord?

They called it waste; she called it gain.
It made them angry; but it made her happy.
They knew the mortal value of her gift,
But she knew the eternal value.
They thought she should've given to some poor;
but she knew to whom her soul's love and devotion belonged.

85

SERVING GOD IN THE FACE OF OPPOSITION

Nehemiah 2:19
They laughed at us and despised us.

Opposition comes in various forms to discourage the child of God from serving God. How do you respond to opposition? How do you overcome opposition?

When Nehemiah embarked on a task to rebuild the wall of Jerusalem, God granted him favour before the king, who gave him all the materials he required. However, two men, Sanballat and Tobiah, set up to discourage Nehemiah and prevent him from accomplishing the task. Satan is also set to intimidate and dissuade you from your task.

Opposition never operates in isolation. It is always targeted against a person's position, stand or task which he or she has purposed to complete. You will never get opposed until you set out to do something significant. What have you set out to do for the Lord?

Those who distract you from your task and service to God will use various means such as distraction, ridicule, mockery, conspiracy, attack, confusion, blackmail and accusation, trickery, deceit, fear and intimidation to stop God's work from moving forward.

Despite the opposition, Nehemiah and the people remained united and continued to work earnestly. With focus and determination, the rebuilding of the wall was successfully completed. Purpose, focus, prayer, faith and determination will keep you on your task until completion. May God grant you the grace to remain focused on the task at hand and to succeed even in the face of opposition.

86

A Channel for God's Blessings

Genesis 12:3
In you, all the families of the earth shall be blessed.

Just as Abraham was a great channel of blessing to all the families of the earth, God wants to make you also a channel of blessing to those around you. We do not choose the family we are born into; however, God has graciously given us the opportunity to be part of a family through who He channels blessings.

It is a privilege to be placed in a family by God. We may not always be proud of our families, but in God's agenda, He has a plan and purpose for all our families. Today, not only do we belong to our human families, we are also members of a spiritual family whose members are connected through our Lord and Savior Jesus Christ. God is counting on us to play our part in building strong families, both natural and spiritual, through which His divine blessings flow.

You are placed in your family for a unique purpose. God's promise was designed to pass from Abraham to Isaac and Jacob and to you and me. We are all part of the covenant blessing. *"And I will make your descendants multiply as the stars of heaven; I will give to your descendants all these lands; and in your seed all the nations of the earth shall be blessed"* (Genesis 26:4).

God's purpose is that people are not isolated. *"God sets the solitary in families" (Psalm 68:6).* He does not want you to feel lonely and forsaken. I do not know the state of your family. I do know that God can work through all that you have been through to bring His blessing to you. Let us remain channels of blessings so that the blessings can flow.

87

A Close Relative

Ruth 4:14
Blessed be the Lord, who has not left you this day without a close relative.

The book of Ruth is a book of love and friendship between a woman and her mother-in-law. In today's world it may seem like a farfetched story or something inconceivable by people. It is also a book of God's love and faithfulness to those who put their trust in him. It is a book of love and redemption.

Life is going to throw its challenges at you. It could be a relationship that is not working, or a debt that you owe. It could be the loss of a loved one, hardship, business failure or the pain of a family torn apart. It could be sickness—physical, emotional or mental. It could be the pain and loneliness that come with loss and bereavement. Though you may not feel God's presence around you, always know that He is still there and will never leave you. In Jesus, we are never alone. He is our close relative.

In Christ Jesus we have a great high priest, friend, brother, advocate, intercessor, Savior, Lord and blessed redeemer. Our one and only true close relative.

God is not finished with you yet. As God turned around Ruth's and Naomi's circumstances, so will He turn your circumstances around for the better. Even when you feel alone, know that God has not left you. He has promised to always be with you. You are not alone. Jesus, our faithful redeemer, is always present.

88

THE EXCELLENCE OF GODLY WISDOM

Proverbs 4:7
Wisdom is the principal thing.

Every child of God needs this God-given wisdom to be fruitful in his life and ministry. Godly wisdom will make you excel in your walk with God and in your relationship with others.

Godly wisdom will guide you into God's will (*Colossians 1:9*). It will enable you to bear godly fruits (*2 Peter 1:5,6,7*). Godly wisdom will help your marriage succeed. Godly wisdom will help you build your home and business (*Proverbs 14:1*). Godly wisdom will cause you to win souls for God's kingdom (*Proverbs 11:30*).

"*Wisdom is the principal thing; therefore, get wisdom: and with all thy getting get understanding*" (*Proverbs 4:7*). Every child of God needs godly wisdom to be able to excel in life. To grow and excel in areas where others have failed, we need godly wisdom.

Jesus Christ, our example and our Savior, exhibited godly wisdom throughout his life. As we reflect today, may we join Solomon to ask for that indispensable treasure, God's divine wisdom. "*Give me now wisdom and knowledge that I may go out and come in before this people*" (*2 Chronicles 1:10*).

Our liberal God has already promised to give wisdom to those who ask. He will give you if you ask Him today. *"If any of you lacks wisdom, let him ask of God, who gives to all liberally and without reproach, and it will be given to him"* *(James 1:5)*.

89

BEWARE OF FALSE TEACHERS

Jude 1:4
For certain men have crept in unnoticed.

In his letter to the believers, Jude warned against the dangers posed by false teachers. He warns that they have crept in unnoticed among God's children. His warning continues to be relevant even today. Many women and young girls have become victims to false teachers, pastors, instructors and prophets which are indeed wolves who appear in sheep's clothing and lure, abuse, hurt, ruin and deceive many. Jude points out some specifics that may help us to identify these bad actors easily. They are immoral and engage in immorality. They neither honour nor respect authority. *"These dreamers defile the flesh, reject authority and speak evil of dignitaries" (Jude 1:8).* Not only are they immoral, these false teachers are also greedy for money. They are also rebellious. *"They have gone in the way of Cain, have run greedily in the error of Balaam for profit and perished in the rebellion of Korah" (Jude 1:11).*

The ability to quickly identify these devious people is one key to avoid the dangers they pose. Another key to avoiding being deceived by such persons is strengthening ourselves in our faith through prayer, effective study of God's word and constant fellowship with God's children.

Never allow yourself to be lured out of fellowship with God's children; instead strive to grow in your faith and knowledge of Christ Jesus. *"But you, beloved, building yourselves up on your most holy faith, praying in the Holy Spirit, keep yourselves in the love of God, looking for the mercy of our Lord Jesus Christ unto eternal life" (Jude 1:20,21).*

90

COVENANT BLESSINGS

Numbers 23:20
He has blessed, and I cannot reverse it.

Rejoice, for you are under God's covenant blessing! When you walk in the ways of God and obey His instructions, you will enjoy His blessings. Balak was afraid of encountering the children of Israel on the battlefield, so he decided to hire a prophet called Balam to curse them. Unfortunately, Balam tried with no success, and upon realizing his mission to curse Israel was fruitless, he made the pronouncement, "He has blessed, and I cannot reverse it." I have good news for you today: when God blesses you, no man can reverse it! Halleluiah!

Stop fighting the enemy physically. We engage in physical fights with the enemy when we do things like fighting our spouse, children, boss, mother-in-law, brothers and sisters. We are reminded that the weapons of our warfare are not carnal.

> *"For the weapons of our warfare are not carnal but mighty in God for pulling down strongholds" (2 Corinthians 10:4).*

As a child of God, you are not alone in this journey of life. You have a covenant blessing. Those who fight you provoke the anger of the Lord. When people rise up against you, they incur the anger of the Lord. You are special. Always remember that no one can curse you when God has blessed you.

The Lord Himself will turn around every curse against you and make it into a blessing instead. He will show Himself strong on your behalf. Rejoice! For you are under God's covenant blessing.

9 1

WHEN JESUS CALLS YOUR NAME

Luke 5: 11
They forsook all and followed Him.

Jesus' ministry was full of touching people's lives. He was a great man who touched the lives of men and women in various ways. Some of those who encountered Him left everything and followed Him.

Every encounter with Jesus offers you an opportunity to accept the call to follow Him. Every experience with Him is an opportunity to let go of the world and follow Him faithfully.

In the story above, Peter offered Jesus his boat to use and teach the crowd; afterward, Jesus directed Peter to cast his net into the sea. Peter knew he and the other fishermen had tried all night and caught nothing. Nonetheless, he chose to obey Jesus, and what followed was a mighty miracle as their net brought in so many fish, they needed help to take them in. Because Peter made his boat available to Jesus, he was a recipient of God's miracle. Your service to God will attract God's blessings to your life. Peter had an opportunity to serve God and he did. That opportunity created an avenue through which Jesus blessed him. Service to God will always create an opportunity for you to be blessed.

Today Jesus is calling you, saying, *"Follow Me."* Will you accept that call? Remember, He is coming back again, and His reward is with Him. There is no better time than now to commit to following the Lord. Jesus is calling you regardless of your race, sex, gender, age or status. Let us, like Peter, forsake the world and follow Him.

92

TOUCHING LIVES, ONE SOUL AT A TIME

John 4:7
Give me a drink.

Jesus' mission on earth was to win us back to God with His love. He desires to touch you and me so we can touch others for Him. Jesus did not only teach and touch people in crowds, but He was also able to reach out, one on one, and touch and restore individual lives.

All around us there are hurting people in need of God's love. They are in our neighbourhoods, at our workplaces and in our churches. To touch others with God's love, we must first experience it ourselves. Jesus was a successful soul-winner. The story of the Samaritan woman teaches us to get to know people and draw them out of their isolation with God's love. *"But he needed to go through Samaria" (John 4:4).* Jesus needed to go through Samaria for a unique purpose. He needed to go through Samaria for the sole purpose of encountering this hurting Samaritan woman and extend God's love to her.

Jesus knows where you are right now in that broken marriage, in that shattered hope, in that mountain of debt, in that guilt of sin. Jesus is not afraid to come where you are. He is not ashamed to be seen with you. He met Zacchaeus in his house full of stolen money. You see, Jesus will meet you where you are, but He will not leave you there!

Like Jesus, we must learn to go out of our way for others. Let us take time to listen to their stories. Let us empathize with their circumstances. Let the love that Jesus showed us shine through us and draw men and women, young and old, rich and poor, to Him.

93

YOU ARE INVITED

Luke 14:18
They all with one accord began to make excuses.

When was the last time you got invited to an event? Here, Jesus begins with lessons on guest etiquette. He then goes on to reveal his ultimate invitation to man. His invitation simply reads, "Follow Me." God has invited us all to be part of the *Marriage Supper of the Lamb*. Have you responded to the invitation?

This invitation to this great event is not ordinary. Some events, like the Olympics, take place every four years, but some invitations are for a once-in-a-lifetime event. Did you ever get invited to a very special event? What if you got an invitation to meet the Queen or the Prime Minister or the President of the United States?

Jesus' invitation is for everyone. Men, women, children, youth, rich, poor, the good and the bad are all welcome. There is something about the call of God; it is open and general, yet it personal and specific. Only you can answer that call for yourself. No one is allowed to represent you. Everyone has been called to salvation through Jesus Christ.

Take note of the timing of this invitation in the Parable of the Great Supper in Luke Chapter 14. It was at suppertime and it was not convenient. No wonder there were many excuses! The first person said, *"I have bought a piece of ground and I must go and see it. I ask you to have me excused" (Luke 14:18)*. The second said, *"I have bought five yoke of oxen,"* and yet the third said, *"I have married a wife, and therefore I cannot come"* *(Luke 14:19, 20)*. Do not let family, business or career hold you back from answering the Lord's invitation. You are invited. What is your response?

94

REJOICE AND BE GLAD!

Philippians 4:4
Rejoice in the Lord always. Again, I will say, rejoice!

Today, the Lord wants you to rejoice and be glad. Do not let worry and anxiety, cares and concerns rob you of the joys of this day. Do not start the day with bitterness of heart or a cold attitude. Start your day with gladness. Begin your morning with rejoicing.

Planning, thinking, and strategizing on your plans are typical everyday actions, but you will agree with me that often we go from planning to worrying and from thinking to panicking. Soon our strength is drained, and the smiles disappear from our faces. If you find that you are often given to worry and anxiety, you are not alone, but the Lord has something better for you. He asks you to come to Him in prayer with your cares and concerns. *"Be anxious for nothing, but in everything by prayer and supplication, with thanksgiving, let your requests be made known to God; and the peace of God, which surpasses all understanding, will guard your hearts and minds through Christ Jesus" (Philippians 4:6, 7).*

One sure way to rejoice in the Lord is always to make time for your personal devotion, where you meditate on God's word and spend time in prayer. You may feel the urge to skip your time of devotion to get to more "important" things on your to-do list, but experience has taught me that taking time to meditate on God's word gives me the grace and strength I need throughout the day. It is okay to leave the dishes in the sink and it's okay to not have everything checked off on your to-do list if you can simply start your day with a personal time with the Lord that He might give you the peace that passes understanding.

95

CONTINUE IN PRAYER

Colossians 4:2
Continue earnestly in prayer.

I know sometimes you feel like you need to take a break from God and from the church. This can happen when we feel overwhelmed with the business of life. But today, I want to encourage you; find time to rest, but don't take a break from God because God never takes a break on you. He is your strength and your hope. Instead, go to Him in prayer and seek His grace to keep you focused on Him, to *continue earnestly in prayer.*

Continue to serve God. Do not stop, do not pause and do not take a break from God; instead, continue serving God, seeking Him and looking up to Him for grace. Let your service to God be done earnestly. That which you do for the Lord, do it with zeal and passion. Is there passion in your prayer? Is there zeal in your service? Is there a purpose, a drive, a passion, an earnestness with which you do the things you do? Are you communicating with God in prayer?

Prayer is your conversations with God. It is the power with which you pull down answers from heaven to earth. Prayer is the key that unlocks heaven's treasures for you. Look at how James describes the power of fervent prayer. *"The effective, fervent prayer of a righteous man avails much"* (James 5:16).

Don't listen to the enemy when he tells you to quit on God. Your life and strength depend on God; therefore, hold on tight to Him. Don't give up. Let us strengthen each other to continue earnestly in prayer until we meet our Lord and Savior Jesus Christ.

96

I HAVE PRAYED FOR YOU

Luke 22:32
But I have prayed for you.

"Simon, Simon! Indeed, Satan has asked for you, that he may sift you as wheat. But I have prayed for you, that your faith should not fail" (Luke 22:31, 32). Notice that Jesus did not say, "I have sent someone to pray for you." Instead, He said, "I have prayed for you."

Oh my dearest Lord and Savior Jesus Christ! That you will pray for me! Thank you for always looking out for me, praying for me, directing, warning, loving and interceding for me.

Child of God, your Savior constantly intercedes for you. Satan's goal is to steal, kill, and to destroy, but Jesus came to give us life and life more abundantly.

It should not come as a surprise that Satan's goal is to harm and destroy you. Our hope lies in Christ, who has come to save us and give us abundant life. *"The thief does not come except to steal, and to kill, and to destroy. I have come that they may have life, and that they may have it more abundantly" (John 10:10).*

I get excited in church when we pray the Lord's prayer and get to the part that says, *"Your Kingdom come. Your will be done. On earth as it is in heaven" (Matthew 6:10).* I use that portion of scripture to pray that no one but Jesus will have my life. I declare and affirm that only God's will be done in my life. Not the will of Satan, nor the will of man or enemies but simply and only the will of God. We know that Satan's plans for us are evil. Only God has the perfect will and best desires for us. We can take comfort in knowing that Jesus has prayed for us.

97

A Grateful Heart

Genesis 14:20
And he gave him a tithe of all.

The key to being a grateful giver of tithes and offerings is having an understanding and a revelation of God as the possessor of heaven and earth and the One who delivers us from troubles. When Abraham returned from rescuing his nephew, Lot, he met Melchizedek, a priest of God. Melchizedek blessed Abram, and in turn, Abram gave him a tithe of all. *"Blessed be Abram of God Most High, Possessor of heaven and earth; And blessed be God Most High, who has delivered your enemies into your hand. And he gave him a tithe of all"* (Genesis 14:19,20).

Abraham understood who his provider was. He had confidence in God as his ultimate source. He knew how far he had come on his journey and he knew who it was that had brought him that far. After Abraham rescued his nephew Lot, along with the men and women who were with him and their goods, the king of Sodom approached him and proposed a deal to Abraham and said, *"Give me the persons and take the goods for yourself."* (Genesis 14:21). But Abraham replied to the king and said, *"I have raised my hand to the Lord, God Most High, the Possessor of heaven and earth, that I will take nothing, from a thread to a sandal strap, and that I will not take anything that is yours, lest you should say, 'I have made Abram rich'"* (Genesis 14:22,23).

Until you have a revelation of who God is, you will struggle with giving your tithes and offerings. No man can outgive God. He is our provision, our protection and our deliverer. He is the Most High God, possessor of heaven and earth.

98

THE GIFTED ARTISANS

Exodus 28:3
So you shall speak to all who are gifted artisans, whom I have filled with the spirit of wisdom.

Your gifts, talents and abilities were given to you by God. He expects you and I to use our gifts and abilities for His good purposes. In today's scripture passage, God was instructing Moses about the garments for the priests. He directed him to speak to all who are gifted artisans, whom He had filled with the spirit of wisdom, to make the priestly garments for Aaron.

We are all gifted differently and uniquely, but the beauty of it is that our gifts are given to us by God for a purpose. When we discover our unique gifts and abilities and use them, we bring glory and honour to God, while blessing those around us. What are your unique abilities? What gifts has God endowed you with? What are those things you are naturally good at? Are you good at singing, dancing, drawing, writing, speaking or acting? Or are you called to fix things, cure people, preach or create new businesses? Do you build structures, build people or raise leaders? There are different kinds of gifts as there are people. There are different kinds of ministries and there are different kinds of activities. What is important is not if yours is considered a gift, or a ministry or an activity; what matters is that we take what God has given us and use it in such a way that those around us are blessed. You too, have your own special gift, ministry, talent, ability or activity. *"There are diversities of gifts, but the same Spirit. There are differences of ministries, but the same Lord. And there are diversities of activities, but it is the same God who works all in all. But the manifestation of the Spirit is given to each one for the profit of all"* 1 Corinthians 12:4,5,6,7)

God expects that you will put the gifts He has given you to use. Like the spiritually gifted artisans who were asked to make Aaron's priestly robes, God is counting on you to put your gifts to good use.

99

THUS FAR

1 Samuel 7:12
Thus far the Lord has helped us.

Today, like Samuel, let us set up a stone of remembrance of the Lord's faithfulness and declare with humble gratitude, "Ebenezer! Thus far the Lord has helped us." Faithful God! Thus far you have helped me. From the time I came into this world, your eyes of mercy have been upon me. You graced me with multiple favours. Favours of health, peace and deliverance. Favours of love, salvation, mercy and redemption.

Thus far, Oh Lord, have you helped me. In laughter and sorrow, through the good times and the bad times. You have fought all my battles and delivered me from all my fears. You have forgiven and still forgive. You have loved and yet continue to love.

When I look back at my life, I can truly say, "Ebenezer! Thus far the Lord has helped me." My strength, my anchor, the One who has said to me multiple times, *"Fear not, for I have redeemed you; I have called you by your name. You are Mine. When you pass through the waters, I will be with you, and through the rivers, they shall not overflow you. When you walk through the fire, you shall not be burned, Nor shall the flame scorch you"* Isaiah *(43:1, 2)*.

Friend, the Lord who has brought you this far will certainly not leave you on your own. He who started that good work in you will be faithful and complete it. Thus far He has brought you and farther still He will guide you until you are safely home in Jesus' bosom, beholding the face of the One who loved you with a perfect love. Reflect, remember and rejoice as you recount the goodness of God in your life. Declare with a heart of joy, *"Thus far the Lord has helped us!" 1 Samuel 7:12*

100

WOMAN, YOU ARE BLESSED.

Luke 1:45
Blessed is she who believed, for there shall be a fulfillment of those
things which were told her from the Lord.

Woman! You are blessed! God has great promises and great plans for you. Your part is simply to believe that He will do what He has promised. What has the Lord said to you? What promises has He made to you through His word?

The scripture today is a Holy Spirit-inspired message from Elizabeth to Mary. "Blessed is she who believed" Why? "for there shall be a fulfillment of those things which were told her from the Lord." The promise is from the Lord. The believing is yours to do. The fulfillment is the Lord's to fulfill.

What promises has God made to you about your life, your marriage, your family, your children, your health, your career, your finances, your future, your ministry and your faith? Have you given up hope of receiving God's blessings for your life?

God has great plans for each one of His children. He wants you to be blessed beyond what you can think or imagine. He tells us that the plans He has for us are good. He plans to give us a future and an expected end. *"For I know the thought that I think toward you, says the Lord, thoughts of peace and not of evil, to give you a future and a hope" (Jeremiah*

29:11). What a great promise to lay hold of. Let us, like Mary, who when the angel broke the good news of God's promise to her, instead of hesitating or disbelieving, declared with a voice of faith and said, *"Behold the maidservant of the Lord! Let it be to me according to your word" (Luke 1:38).*

About the Author

Eziaku Odimuko is a creative writer who is passionate about inspiring and empowering everyone around her. She is an author, banker, mom, daughter and Pastor's wife. She has served alongside her husband in ministry for seventeen years and has successfully led a fifteen-year banking career.

A loving and passionate voice on love, courtship and marriage, Eziaku's first book, *Relationship Smart,* was published in 2014. It gives guidance and help to women of all ages as they navigate the world of marriage and relationships.

Eziaku has a people-centered approach to everything she does. Wherever she finds herself, at work, at church or in her community, Eziaku is all about helping people find the help they need with their finances, relationships, or faith.

She regularly hosts singles and marriage relationship seminars where she gives practical ideas to help strengthen marriages and families. She also has an online network, *Share Hearts Women,* through which she writes inspirational articles.

With her second book, *Brighter Days,* Eziaku shares her collection of personal inspirational thoughts and meditations to bring hope, love and blessings to everyone.

She and her husband, Dike, are blessed with three beautiful daughters, Abigail, Esther and Sarah. They live in Edmonton, Alberta.

EZYODIMUKO

EZYODIMUKO

EZYODIMUKO

EZYODIMUKO

WWW.EZYODIMUKO.COM/BOOKS

WWW.EZYODIMUKO.COM

SAYHELLO@ EZYODIMUKO.COM

Made in the USA
Columbia, SC
29 May 2021